Taking America Off Drugs

Taking America Off Drugs

*Why Behavioral Therapy is More Effective
for Treating ADHD, OCD, Depression,
and Other Psychological Problems*

Stephen Ray Flora

State University of New York Press

Published by
State University of New York Press, Albany

For information, contact State University of New York Press, Albany, NY
www.sunypress.edu

Cover photo copyright Firebrandphotography/Dreamstime.com

Production by Michael Haggett
Marketing by Fran Keneston

Library of Congress Cataloging-in-Publication Data

Flora, Stephen Ray, 1963–
    Taking america off Drugs : why behavioral therapy is more effective for treating
ADHD, OCD, depression, and other psychological problems / Stephen Ray Flora.
        p. cm.
    Includes bibliographical references.
    ISBN 978–0–7914–7189–0 (hardcover : alk. paper)
    ISBN 978–0–7914–7190–6 (pbk. : alk. paper)
    1. Behavior therapy. 2. Neurobehavioral disorders—Chemotherapy.
3. Psychotropic drugs. I. Title.

RC489.B4F56 2007
616.89'142—dc22

                                                                                        200636595

10 9 8 7 6 5 4 3 2 1

Contents

Chapter 1

Introduction
The Drug Deception

THE DECEPTION

America has been deceived—deceived by the drug companies, by psychiatry, by our children's teachers, by well-meaning physicians, and by mental health workers of all stripes. The deception has been so complete and successful that Americans believe the deception is fact. As a result of this deception, Americans are suffering.

The deception is that whatever one's problem—hyperactivity, short attention span, depression, shyness, sadness, obsessive-compulsive disorder (OCD), phobias, anxiety, panic, overeating, sexual dysfunction, poor athletic performance, sleeping difficulties, drug abuse, irritable bowel syndrome, and even schizophrenia, to name a few—there is a drug that can help the problem, if not cure it. But to keep the current customer base, the drug companies do not really want to permanently solve the problem. Rather, they want to keep selling Americans drugs. The drug deception is now widely entrenched, thus those with behavioral problems have been so completely fooled that they are now unknowingly reinforcing the deception. The deception has become self-perpetuating. In fact, many with behavioral problems and their advocates do not even consider their behavioral difficulties *behavioral*. No, they believe it is "fact" that their problems are "neurochemical" or "brain based." And if a problem is assumed to be neurochemically, brain based (although behavioral problems are not), then a logical—but often an incorrect—assumption is that the best way to help the problem is with chemicals, with drugs.

1

It is the nature of deceptions that they are believed to be true by those deceived. This is the case with the mental health community. The mental health community—the "professionals" and patients—has so completely bought the drug companies' and psychiatry's sales pitch that behavioral problems are "brain disorders," that now it too is perpetuating the deception. I was invited to be on the speakers' bureau of a local mental health organization "funded by a grant from the Ohio Department of Mental Health." Included in its mailing to me was the flier "Some Facts about Mental Illness," which included the statements: "Mental illnesses are disorders of the brain that disrupt a person's thinking, feeling, moods, and ability to relate to others.... Just as diabetes is a disorder of the pancreas, mental illnesses are brain disorders.... As a diabetic takes insulin, most people with serious mental illness need medication to help control symptoms." These "facts," and the logic behind them, are wrong.

The truth is, behavioral problems are *behavioral*. It is, the behavior that is dysfunctional and causing distress. A "chemical imbalance" in a person's brain does not cause most of these problems; rather, it is a behavioral imbalance. Or, as one child being screened for attention deficit disorder (ADD) told his doctor: "It's not a chemical imbalance, Dr. Diller—it's a *living* imbalance" (Diller, 1998, italics in original). Troublesome behavior causes troublesome feelings and may result in atypical chemical and neurological profiles more often than any supposed chemical imbalance causes troublesome behavior and feelings. That is, when behavior is out of balance, the body, including the brain, gets out of balance, and when behavior becomes more balanced, the body, including brain chemistry, returns to normal. Furthermore, behavioral treatments are almost always more effective, and more widely beneficial, than drug treatments. Behavioral treatments have advantages that drug treatments do not, and drug treatments have disadvantages that behavioral treatments do not.

Study after study will prove that behavioral treatment is more effective than drug treatment for behavioral problems. In a *minority* of cases for a *minority* of behavioral difficulties, drug treatment may be necessary, but only in combination with behavioral treatment.

However, profits, political lobbying, and marketing directed at America's quick-fix, fast-paced, immediate gratification-oriented culture have proven to be more powerful than careful, unbiased, outcome-based scientific research. The drug companies understand that children, parents, and others prefer, and are more likely to be influenced by, superheroes, comic books, and warm stories than they are by a scientific report. Superheroes, comic books, and warm stories are exactly what the drug companies are using to promote their drugs. In September 2001, just in time for the school year, the drug companies began to market their amphetamines (or closely related drugs) for children targeted directly at parents in leading magazines, including *Parents, Parenting*, and *Reader's Digest*, to name a few. The "soaps" (TV soap operas) might now more accurately be called the "drugs," because the advertisements have shifted from household cleaning products to drug solicitations.

But there may still be time to keep everyone on earth from being drugged. Some concerned professionals and parents are not swallowing the drug companies' would-be cure-all (e.g., Antonuccio, 1995; Diller, 1998). In almost all cases, safe, effective behavioral treatments exist for "mental disorders," psychological maladjustments, and behavioral difficulties. If effective nondrug alternatives exist, then why are they not more widely used and promoted? There are several reasons for the current state of affairs.

DRUGS, THE FALSE PROMISES

When we are sick, we go to the doctor and we expect him or her to give us something to make us feel better. We expect to be cured. If we went home with nothing, we would feel cheated. Now that America believes that behavioral problems are diseases—brain disorders and chemical imbalances—when Americans go to a mental health professional they expect to be given something that will cure them. Doctors are more than willing to oblige. Many give amphetamines prescriptions for children based merely on one 15-minute consultation with parents (Diller, 1998). Patients and parents may feel cheated if instead of being given pills to "cure" the problem they were given homework exercises and firm advice on systematic, consistent, large-scale changes in their daily lives that may be necessary in order to live with and manage the behavioral difficulty. Given the desire for an easy, immediate quick fix, many reject the behavioral approach and seek out someone who will give them drugs. But the drug "quick fix" is a delusion, because for many psychological difficulties, behavioral treatments will produce beneficial results faster than drug treatment will.

For many real diseases—strep throat, flu, bacterial infections—vaccines can prevent or drugs can permanently treat, if not cure, the illnesses.

But despite claims to the contrary, there are no drug "cures" for behavioral problems. In the mid-1990s The Learning Channel (TLC) ran an episode on "out-of-control" behaviors on its show *The Human Condition*. One mother of a teenager with OCD claimed that her daughter was "cured" with "just two pills." The mother said that she wanted "buckets and buckets" of the drug (Prozac), and that the drug was "always" going to be in the house. This is a sad story, for without behavioral therapy, if the teen ever does go without drugs, relapse will occur, and the OCD may very well be worse than if no drugs had ever been taken. But behavioral therapy produces lasting change in OCD and other behavioral problems. The teen was not cured; her problem was just temporarily suppressed with drugs. For behavioral problems to be "cured," rather than drugging the individual, the actual behaviors of the individual must be addressed. Unnecessarily putting people on drugs for life keeps them from living—from experiencing life completely. It is unethical and disgraceful. Drugging people keeps them from experiencing the natural highs and lows of life.

Crutch

In addition to real physical dependency (such as my morning coffee) that may result after years of unnecessary drug use or abuse, drugs often become a lifetime crutch for behavioral problems that could have been effectively treated and managed without drug use. As a result of years of doctor-prescribed drug use, psychological patients come to believe, like other drug addicts, that they cannot function without their daily fix. In this case, drugs do not solve behavioral problems, they only create more.

Rebound

If a psychological problem is fully treatable with a behavioral approach, *without any drugs*, then drug treatment is obviously unnecessary. But if a drug treatment is stopped, then a behavioral rebound is likely, and the problem appears worse than it ever was before drug treatment. This rebound, or "contrast effect," strengthens the illusion that drugs are necessary. For example, a family member may argue: "She got worse when we took her off medication. Therefore, we need to keep her on drugs. Furthermore [it may be falsely argued], since she got worse when she went off the medication, it proves the problem is biological, nothing we can do."

Placebo and Expectancy Effects

Many people who are given a sugar pill (placebo) and told it will improve sexual or athletic performance report that their sexual or athletic performance did in fact improve. Physicians have been aware for centuries of the power of these expectancy and placebo effects. Placebo effects have been a cornerstone of both medicine and quackery for as long as the fields have existed.

For example, antibiotics kill bacteria, but they have *no* effect on viral infections. Despite the fact that they have no effect, many people *insist* that their doctors give them antibiotics for viral infections such as colds. The doctors know that the prescription drug will not affect the virus causing the cold, but the patient leaves the office feeling satisfied. And when the body's immune system naturally fights off the virus, the patient falsely attributes feeling better to the drug. (Unfortunately, the practice of prescribing unnecessary antibiotics is resulting in drug-resistant bacteria and is becoming a serious public health concern.) If people believe alcohol causes uninhibited behavior and they are led to believe that they have drunk alcohol then they act less inhibited, even if they actually consumed no alcohol (e.g., Wilson, 1981). People often behave in accordance to expectations. This effect reveals another danger of labeling people with "mental disorders" and claiming they are "brain disorders." For example, a child labeled with ADD may believe that he is supposed to act "out of control" and misbehave. It is a brain disorder after all, not Johnnie's fault that he hit Susie. The ADD child is *expected* to act that way.

Likewise, instead of learning social skills and public speaking skills (behaviors), a person who gets nervous speaking in public (as most humans naturally do) can be labeled a "social phobic." Now the *behavioral problem* falsely becomes a *brain disorder*; the would-be speaker is expected to act that way. And since social phobia is a brain disorder "brought on" by fear of public speaking, then it becomes acceptable to avoid public speaking or to take drugs, likely Prozac or another selective serotonin reuptake inhibitor (SSRI), if the "brain-disordered" person must speak in public. Are we really ready to accept that people who get excessively nervous when speaking in public have a brain disorder requiring drugs? Or can we accept that the person has a behavioral difficulty that can be addressed head-on and overcome with some effort and *without* any drugs?

Expectancy effects not only influence the person taking the substance or treatment but influence those around the person as well. For example, there is absolutely no evidence that refined sugar increases "hyperactivity" in children. Yet the urban myth continues. When adults believe that children have eaten sugar, *the adult's behavior changes*! Any changes, increased "hyperactivity" by the child who eats sugar, are more likely due to the changed behavior and statements of the adults, not the sugar itself. In short, many "improvements" from taking drugs, rather than "prove" the problem is due to a brain chemical disorder, are simply placebo or expectancy effects, and they usually are only temporary.

Remission

Whether or not one gets a drug, placebo, or nothing, many, if not most, behavioral and psychological problems will get better without any formal treatment whatsoever. For example, even in cases of severe depression, the probability of remission is close to 90% (Thase, 1990). When the depressive situation, the stressful life situation that precipitates the depression, is improved, when the living of life is reengaged, then the depression will lift.

In fact, spontaneous remission and placebo effects account for recent research results falsely heralded as evidence that drug treatment can "cure" depression. A team of researchers led by psychiatrist A. John Rush reported that one third of patients were helped by the antidepressant Celexa, meaning, of course, that two thirds were not helped by the drug. But if the patients who did not respond on the first drug were put on another drug after 14 weeks, about one third of those initially nonimproving patients improved. In all, about 50% of the patients improved after being but on one or more drugs. "After unsuccessful treatment with an SSRI [antidepressant drug], approximately one in four patients had a remission of symptoms after switching to another antidepressant" (Rush, Trivedi, Wisniewski et al., 2006, p. 1231). The message pushed in the press was: Take drugs, and if that does not work, take more drugs! "The big message is that symptoms can be eliminated in over 50% of people who receive two [drug] treatment steps," Rush proclaimed at a news conference. "Most patients should expect at least two [drug] treatment attempts to become asymptomatic" (quoted from DeNoon, March 22, 2006, p. 1).

These results are invalid, because the Rush et al. 2006 study included no placebo control group. In other words, it is just as likely that as many, or more, patients would have improved if they had been switched to an inert sugar pill instead of another drug. Rates on remission also inform us that many patients' depression would have lifted without any treatment whatsoever. This information is available but conveniently ignored by those advocating drug use.

Arif Khan, S. Khan, and Walter Brown of the Northwest Clinical Research Center examined clinical trial data of the nine antidepressant drugs approved by the FDA between 1985 and 2000, comprising 10,030 patients, and the 13 anxiolytic drugs (anti-anxiety drugs) approved by the FDA between 1985 and 2000, comprising 8,340 patients (2002). Fewer than half of the drugs in either class were any better than placebo. "These data suggest that conventional psychopharmacologic treatments for depression and anxiety are superior to placebo less than half the time and call into serious question the widely propagated notion that placebo controls can be dispensed within clinical trials of these agents. Exclusion of placebo controls in favor of noninferiority trials would result in a high likelihood that ineffective antidepressants and anxiolytics would be foisted on the public" (2002, p. 193). But this is exactly what is happening. Irving Kirsch and his colleagues conducted a similar analysis of the 6 most widely prescribed antidepressant drugs, and they reached the same conclusion. "Approximately 80% of the response to medication was duplicated on placebo control groups.... If drug and placebo effects are additive, *the pharmacological effects of antidepressants are clinically negligible*" (Kirsch, Moore, Sloboria, & Nicholls, 2002, italics added). These results allow two conclusions, which are further developed in the book. First, antidepressant drugs and anti-anxiety drugs do not help problems such as depression or anxiety (but behavioral treatments do). Second, America's drug deception is deepened by studies that do not use placebo controls or take into account naturally occurring rates of remission.

RESPONSIBILITY AND GUILT

Convincing people that behavioral problems are physical ones, "brain based," has been an easy sell, because it frees the individual, the individual's family, loved ones, teachers, coworkers, and employers from responsibility and guilt. It is no longer the child's, parents', or teachers' fault or responsibility that a child has no social skills, is behind academically, and is rude and aggressive. No, it is a brain disorder—have a pill. And even though there is no replicable scientific evidence that any "symptoms" of attention deficit or hyperactivity or aggression are caused by a chemical or structural imbalance in the brain, if one drug does not work, then others will be tried until the "imbalance" is corrected—until the child is drugged into compliance and complacency. If office workers or students get so nervous that they vomit, faint, or shake when they try to go to the office or school, then it is not because they are teased, harassed, overworked, or tormented at the office or school—"No, no," say the drug industry and psychiatry, "they have a chemical imbalance. Give them an 'anti-anxiety' drug." Because they supposedly suffer from a brain disorder, society is freed of guilt in establishing the environmental conditions creating the anxiety. Since the problem is falsely labeled "brain disorder," society has no responsibility to change the conditions responsible for the anxiety (the condition is argued to be in the brain, not the external environment).

REALITY

The truth, uncomfortable as it may be, is that problems in an individual's family, social, school, or work environment *are mainly responsible* for behavioral difficulties. For example, *U.S. News and World Report* writer Susan Brink reports: "Severe depression in a very young child is almost always caused by a major upheaval. 'In kids under 5, it's marital discord, divorce, witnessing violence,' says Glen Elliott, director of child and adolescent psychiatry at the University of California-San Francisco. A pill won't help. The daunting solution is to change family life or move from a dangerous neighborhood" (March 6, 2000, p. 49). In *Enjoy Old Age,* the late Harvard behaviorist B. F. Skinner gives the same advice. You may be depressed "simply because you can no longer do many of the things you have enjoyed. Perhaps you have liked talking to people but now there is no one to talk to. Perhaps you have enjoyed the countryside but are now cooped up in the city. Finding someone to talk to or some way of getting to the countryside will be better than remaining alone in the city taking Valium [or Prozac, Paxil, or another drug of your choice]" (Skinner & Vaughan, 1987, p. 118). Unfortunately, it is easier, and often a cop-out, to drug young and old individuals who have behavioral problems than it is to address the environmental conditions that produce the problems. The reality is, dysfunctional behaviors are a product of dysfunctional contingencies in a person's environment.

WORK AND HAPPINESS

People with behavioral difficulties and those who care about them must determine what a meaningful solution is worth to them. To overcome the dysfunctional, abnormal, troublesome behaviors, a person's dysfunctional contingencies must be changed. Most things in life that are worthwhile require some effort. Behavioral treatments often require some effort by both the people with problems and their families, teachers, employers, coworkers, and/or classmates. But drug therapy requires virtually no effort—reflecting its ultimate worth for most behavioral problems. By drugging children into compliance and docility, or by drugging adults into comfortable numbness, drug therapies work *around* the problem. But behavioral approaches work *on* or *at* the actual problem. They attack the problem—whereas drug approaches hide the problem.

Unfortunately, large portions of society have developed an aversion to work (Eisenberger, 1989). The "me generation" and "generation X" have been taught to expect immediate gratification and happiness as a birthright. They are told in song, "Don't worry, be happy." But there are things all people should worry about: their families, their country, their job, their academic performance. Many in society, perhaps a majority of "mental health professionals," now believe that all such worry is wrong. Rather than address, attack, or work directly on the sources of worry, such as problematic family, work, or school situations, Americans are expected to take a drug to mask the problem or to feel good despite it. As Skinner noted: "Americans take billions of pills every year to feel better about their lives even when their lives remain wretched" (Skinner & Vaughan, 1987, p. 118).

Happiness is not always a natural state of being or a U.S. birthright. Americans are guaranteed freedom of the *pursuit* of happiness. Happiness itself is not guaranteed. Biological psychiatry and the drug companies want Americans to pursue happiness in a pill. Of course, that is one possible and often-taken approach—with both legal and illegal drugs. But most *successful pursuits require planning, effort, and execution*—that is, the behavioral approach to happiness. Furthermore, while many drugs are very efficient at making people feel good, "feeling good" is just part of *being happy.* The journey, pursuit, effort, and *behavior* make people happy and make them feel good. Feeling good while one's behavior remains dysfunctional and one's life remains wretched is not happiness. Drugged people cannot feel happiness anymore than they can feel pain. An absence of pain does not equal happiness.

THE FALSE DRUG SOLUTIONS

Despite their vast differences, for the spectrum of behavioral difficulties and "mental illnesses," all claimed to be caused by neurological-chemical imbalances, the same three general drug "treatments" are offered. Major tranquilizers and "antipsychotic" or "neuroleptic" medications such as chlorpromazine (Thorazine), haloperidol (Haldol), and thioridazine (Mellaril) are given to people to "treat" such widely different problems as schizophrenia, retardation, autism, and other severe but *nonrelated* problems. But other than sedating the patient (the victim?) and making the patient "more manageable," little is actually known about how these powerful and dangerous medications affect the person taking them (Gelman, 1999). Because the tranquilizers are so powerful, "minor" tranquilizers were developed. These "minor" tranquilizers, including alprazolam (Xanax), buspirone (Buspar), and diazepam (Valium), are referred to as "sedative hypnotics" and are often used to "treat" depression and behaviors associated with excessive anxiety. As the name suggests, they "sedate" or "hypnotize," but they do not address the causes or sources of the depression and anxiety (e.g., marital, family, or employment problems).

The monoamines are a class of neurotransmitters (chemicals released by one neuron to communicate with other neurons) generally associated with pleasure and arousal. The monoamines include serotonin, dopamine, epinephrine, and norepinephrine (the latter two formerly were called adrenaline and noradrenaline, and the phrase "to get your adrenaline pumping" accurately describes the generally pleasurable arousal produced by their increased activity). Several major classes of psychiatric drugs function to increase the activity of the monoamines. Like the tranquilizers, these drugs are given for a wide range of vastly different behavioral problems. Adderall, Ritalin, and other stimulant drugs are chemicals that are, or just slight modifications of, amphetamines. As the name suggests, the biological function of amphetamine-like drugs is to *amplify* the mono*amine* systems. The older antidepressants, tricyclic antidepressants, and monoamine oxidase inhibitors also work to increase monamine activity.

In addition to the amphetamines and closely related drugs given to children and adults who have been labeled with "attention-deficit hyperactivity disorder" (ADHD) the so-called "miracle" drugs of the psychiatric-pharmaceutical conglomerate are the SSRIs. Popular brand names include Prozac, Paxil, Louvox, and Zoloft. The SSRIs work *selectively* on *serotonin* (a monoamine) to *inhibit* its *reuptake* by the neuron that released it, thereby increasing serotonin's effects. Serotonin's effects are vast, and complex, and much remains a mystery. Broadly, and often inaccurately, described as a "mood regulator," serotonin is involved in at least six major brain circuits involving almost all of the major structures of the brain, and there are at least 15 different serotonin receptors, all with different functions (Barlow & Durand, 1999). Thus although "SSRI" sounds scientifically specific, taking SSRIs amounts to a general chemical whitewashing of the brain and is associated with a wide range of side effects, from sexual dysfunction to indigestion to insomnia. Yet SSRIs are promoted as being specifically targeted for everything from eating disorders to depression to common phobias. This excessive drugging must be questioned.

Nevertheless, the American appetite for legal and illegal drugs grows unabated. This appetite is not without consequence.

THE DISGRACE

According to the National Association of Chain Drug Stores, the number of prescriptions filled has risen by more than 50%, to over 3 billion prescriptions since 1992 (Readers Digest, June 2001, p. 38), but has Americans' mental or physical health improved 50% since then? No. If enough money is involved, even the most ethical people can be tempted to bend their morals. Doctors and researchers are no exception. It is a conflict of interest for a stockbroker to recommend a stock he or she owns and unethical to recommend the stock at all unless interests are disclosed to the public. Likewise, it is a conflict of interest for a "scientific" researcher to promote a drug therapy if the researcher has financial interests in the company that makes the drug in question. It is unethical not to disclose such a conflict of interest, but this is exactly what frequently happens with regard to drug therapy. In an internal audit published in

February 2000, *The New England Journal of Medicine* editors found that 19 out of 40 drug therapy reviews failed to disclose the researchers' drug company support. If a leading journal in medical ethics regularly publishes such conflict of interest reports without acknowledging the conflict, then it is reasonable to expect that the less prestigious journals are publishing even more biased, questionable reports as unbiased "scientific" findings.

For the drug companies, business is business. The goal is to make money, not to help people—if they help, fine, but helping is clearly secondary, and ethics is a distant afterthought. The Immune Response Corporation paid researchers at the University of California-San Francisco (UCSF) to conduct studies on its proposed HIV drug. The researchers published their findings in *The Journal of the Medical Association*, showing that the drug was no more effective than a placebo in reducing AIDS or mortality. A sugar pill is as good as the drug. The company's response was not to try to develop drugs that would be effective—no, the response was to sue UCSF for damages and withhold data and blood samples from the researchers! (The suit has been settled.) According to Dr. Drummond Remune, a medical professor at UCSF not involved in the study, drug companies try to withhold data "for commercial reasons only." Dr. Remune said: "We are trying to get across to companies that if they are going to pay for research, they have to live with the results. It is just as important to know that something doesn't work as that it does" (from Guterman & Van Der Werf, 2001, p. A29). But if the doctors and the public learn that something does not work, then profits decrease. Thus the companies try to withhold data and sue researchers for being objective and honest.

Drugs are dangerous. Up to 100,000 people die each year because of medical mistakes, but that many people *several times over die from drug complications*. Pharmacologist Joe Graedon and medical anthropologist Teresa Graedon, Ph.D., report: "Physicians, nurses and pharmacists are not required to disclose drug complications. If anything, there is a disincentive to acknowledge problems because of a fear of legal action.... Experts estimate that 2 million people are hospitalized because of their medicines, but only 33,500 cases are reported" (Graedon & Graedon, 2000a, p. A4).

Despite these dangers, drugs are increasingly pushed, not only on adults but on children, pets, and even on children's fictional characters! The *Canadian Medical Association Journal* published a report recommending medication for Winnie the Pooh and his friends (Shea,

Gordon, Hawkins, Kawchuk, & Smith, 2000). Although the report was supposedly tongue in cheek, the recommendation is seriously sobering: Drug them all! "Pooh needs intervention," the authors state. Do they recommend assertiveness training, role playing, or other skill-building interventions? No. "We feel drugs are in order" (Shea et al., 2000, p. 1557). Ritalin, an amphetamine-like drug, is recommended for Pooh. Not only is Pooh supposedly suffering from ADHD, but like all good storybook bears, because Pooh thinks about honey, he supposedly suffers from OCD too. The donkey Eeyore, is said to need an antidepressant such as fluoxetine (e.g., Prozac) and Piglet on antianxiety narcotic medication. Reflecting the ignorance of the drug approach, the authors cannot agree on how to drug Tigger the tiger—some want stimulant medication, Ritalin or other amphetamines, while others argue for a psychiatric sedative. The article is sobering, and revealing, because all of the authors are physicians specializing in pediatrics or neurology. The authors ignore behavioral therapy and agree that medication is necessary, but they argue for medications that have the opposite effects for the same problem! That is like looking for solutions to pollution at the center of the earth or in outer space but ignoring what goes on the earth's surface. Equally troublesome is the implication that individuality is not valued—all should be drugged until all are average.

Why drug a character such as Tigger, who is happy, curious, and full of childlike energy and wonder? Because he is not *average*? If your child is happy, curious, and full of childlike energy and wonder, should he or she be drugged because of not being *average*? So what if Pooh is more mild mannered than average, and so what if he likes honey? Is Pooh not a warm, affectionate, giggly companion to his human friend Christopher Robin? Should we drug children who are more mild mannered and affectionate than average or who have acute interests? Apparently anything that is not "average" has become a disorder requiring medication. Is individuality a disorder now? The very meaning of average means that 50% will be below and 50% above; 50% of people will be more active than others, and 50% will be less active; 50% will be able to concentrate longer, and 50% will concentrate less; 50% will get more nervous when speaking in public, and so on. Do we drug everybody into bland sameness? Of course, when a person is so far from average on a *behavioral* characteristic that it causes personal distress or an inability to function at work, school, or socially, then the behavior should be addressed. That does not mean, however, that the individual should be drugged. Yet drugging ourselves into bland sameness is exactly what Americans are doing.

The "diagnostic criteria" of mental disorders are so (purposefully?) vague that virtually every human has some sort of "mental disorder," or at least suffers from several symptoms, thus every individual in the world is a good candidate for one drug "treatment" or another. For example, the criteria for ADHD include: "Often fidgets with hands or feet or squirms in seat. Often talks excessively. Often blurts out answers before questions have been completed. Often has difficulty waiting in turn." What *normal, healthy* child does *not* do these things? My youngest brother now holds a Ph.D. in quantitative psychology from the University of North Carolina. He was a double major (math and psychology) at Kenyon College. He has worked as a statistical consultant on several top research and business projects. However, as a child, during dinner he did not squirm in his seat; he simply refused to sit in his seat—*period*. He ate meals standing up, *next* to his seat, not in it. Should my parents have drugged him so that he would sit in his seat without squirming, or should they have allowed his atypical, nonaverage standing-while-eating behavior? Drugs could have suppressed his standing during meals, but what else would they have suppressed?

A pamphlet promoting the drug Paxil for "social anxiety disorder" states that "some of the signs and symptoms include": 'The anxiety-provoking social situation may cause physical symptoms like blushing, sweating, shaking, trembling, tense muscles, shaky voice, dry mouth or a pounding heart'" (GlaxoSmithKline, 2001). What completely *normal* person has *not* experienced these things before and during social situations—before or during a meeting with the boss, clients, student body, or faculty, or even asking a date to the prom. If one did *not* experience any "blushing, sweating, shaking, trembling, tense muscles, shaky voice, dry mouth or a pounding heart," then *that would be abnormal*! Psychiatry and the drug companies are trying to convince the world that normal, albeit sometimes uncomfortable, but normal nevertheless, behaviors and feelings are abnormal and require medication.

We have been led down a slippery slope of labels. What used to be called appropriately and simply a behavioral problem or difficulty came to be a labeled a "behavioral disorder." "Disorders" are not very different from, or a result of, "diseases." Almost overnight, simple behavior problems became "brain diseases." Americans have been long conditioned to believe that the best way to treat a disease is with drugs, so that is what we are now doing for problem behavior.

SHAME

"Paxil, Prozac, Ritalin. . . . Are These Drugs Safe for Kids?" asks the cover of the March 6, 2000, *U.S. News & World Report*. In some cases the answer is "we don't know if the drugs are safe for children, but we medicate millions of children anyway," and in other cases the answer is "no, the drugs are not safe, but we medicate millions of children anyway." (We want them to act "average" after all.) Americans are drugging their children with psychiatric drugs as soon as they learn to talk and walk! The *U.S. News'* cover story, "The Perils of Pills: The Psychiatric Medication of Children Is Dangerously Haphazard," was in part a response to findings reported in the *Journal of the American Medical Association* (Zito, Safer, dosReis, Gardner, Boles, & Lynch (2000, pp. 1025–1030), "that the number of 2-to-4-year-old children on Ritalin, antidepressants, and other psychoactive drugs increased dramatically from 1991 through 1995. Startling as it is, the news about toddlers merely underscores the rise in the use of powerful psychiatric drugs in kids of all ages—despite the fact that these drugs are largely untested for use in the young" (Shute, Locy, & Pasternak, March 6, 2000, p. 45). Furthermore, the reporters continue, "The treatment children get is often dangerously haphazard. Some are medicated, with no follow-up" (p. 45). This program of treatment often causes more problems than it solves, especially when a poor diagnosis results in putting a child on medication that only compounds the problem: For example, a girl is given no counseling for her father's death but instead is put on the very same drug her father was on when he committed suicide. The drug's listed side effects include "paranoid reactions, antisocial behavior, trouble concentrating, and hostility." A 7-year-old girl, later diagnosed with bipolar disorder, was put on the amphetamine-like Ritalin (a very inappropriate drug for bipolar disorder) and took a butcher knife to her sister. A depressed 16-year-old who was given Paxil and told there was no need to visit again for 3 weeks stabs his grandmother to death 61 times (Shute et al., 2000).

Drugging children, especially babies, for nonaverage behavior is particularly troubling, for two reasons. First, because many of the drugs have not been tested on youngsters, it is simply not known what effects drugging them will have—in the short term or in the long run. But, second, it is known that children are not simply small adults. Animal studies repeatedly reveal that many of the medications given for behavioral problems *permanently* change (damage) the developing nervous system. "Almost nothing is known about how antidepressants and other psychoactive drugs affect a child's developing brain" (Shute et al., 2000, p. 47).

Chapter 2

The Behavioral Balance

THE BEHAVIORAL SOLUTION

Fortunately, in addition to bringing to light the excessive practice of drugging America's children, a *U.S. News & World Report's* article (Shute et al., 2000) pointed to the behavioral solution:

> All too often, children get drugs with none of the behavior modification, counseling, and long-term follow-up that mental health experts say are essential.... But even the pharmaceutical companies say it is inappropriate to prescribe anti-depressants for children without exploring other methods of treatment, particularly behavioral therapy... in elevating [presumed] biological causes of mental disorders, society risks ignoring other key factors: family, environment, culture. If a child behaves badly because the parents' marriage is in turmoil, is the problem with the child or with the family? Are today's parents too busy to give difficult children the one-on-one attention and patience they need? Do teachers demand that children be drugged rather than accept a rambunctious classroom? (pp. 48–50)

The behavioral treatment is basic but very effective, as reporter Susan Brink (2000) notes:

> Behavioral therapy can help when a child, even a preschooler, has attention-deficit hyperactivity disorder.... The therapy is

a consistent system of rewards and consequences. "You catch them being good, you praise them and give lots of rewards," said Bruce Black, a child psychiatrist in Wellesley, Mass. If they're bad, a parent gives them a timeout or takes away a toy. Children with obsessive-compulsive disorder can benefit from behavioral therapy as well as exposure therapy. If a girl feels a need to constantly wash after touching a toy that she fears is dirty, or just plain yucky, she might be led to touch the toy and taught relaxation techniques to ease anxiety. (p. 49)

Comparisons

The superiority of the behavioral approach over the drug approach for behavioral problems can best be seen by taking major behavioral problems and comparing the two approaches on a problem-by-problem basis. The use and abuse of muscle-building steroids serve as a useful introduction to the comparative approach this book will take.

Questions that athletes and millions of normal teenage boys ask include: How strong is strong enough? How fast is fast enough? How long a recovery is long enough? How far from average must one's strength, speed, and recovery time be until it is "abnormal"? How far from average must strength, speed, and recovery be before medical intervention is acceptable? How far from elite performance must one be before medical intervention is acceptable? Is it ever?

Anabolic steroids, natural or synthetic androgenic (male) hormones, increase muscle size, strength, speed, and aggression and decrease recovery time following workouts. In some cases, such as severe atrophy following an accident, steroids are medically useful and perhaps life saving. But the vast majority of steroid use and abuse occurs simply to improve athletic performance or one's looks. "The appetite for these drugs is a product of our culture's obsession with muscularity and athletic success for males," according to Pennsylvania State University's Charles E. Yesalis. Furthermore, states Yesalis, "The steroid problem has been known about in professional sports for at least two decades, and in high school for at least one decade . . . young people's appetite for steroids actually increased after Ben Johnston got caught in 1988. They saw that Johnston blew [U.S. sprinter] Carl Lewis away when Johnson was on steroids" (quoted in Bower, 1991, p. 31). While drugs can improve perfromance, changing behaviors also can improve athletic performance and one's looks as well. What are the differences between steroids (i.e., drugs) and behavior modification?

Ease

Increases in muscle speed, strength, and size are only a pill or an injection away with steroids. Behaviors necessary for increases in muscle speed, strength, and size include regular, often intense, training and changes in eating, sleeping, and drinking habits. All are difficult to accomplish.

Speed of Results

Steroid drugs produce results almost immediately. Results from behavior modification to improve performance may not be noticed for months or even years. But there is a steep price for easy, quick, and performance-and look-enhancing steroid drug use. The price includes male breasts, acne, and shriveled testicles for starters. Unless one remains on steroids for life (a very *unwise* course of action), because the drug injections give the body its testosterone, the testes may stop producing hormones of their own and simply shrivel up. Because the drug injections throw the body's hormone system into a spin when drug use is stopped, many female characteristics may become pronounced. The late, great, professional football player, Lyle Alzato blamed his brain cancer and early death on steroid, growth hormone, and amphetamine abuse. Contrast effects also occur where performance is worse once a user goes off the drugs than if the drugs had never been taken in the first place. One also may add sexual erectile failure to the list of performance problems.

In "Sexual Functioning of Male Anabolic Steroid Abusers" (1993), Howard Moss, M.D., George Panzak, R.N., and Ralph Tarter, Ph.D., of the University of Pittsburgh School of Medicine found that using steroids is not a good thing to do. Male bodybuilders on steroids have significantly more trouble achieving an erection compared to those who are not on steroids. Additionally, in comparing bodybuilders who never used steroids to current steroid users and former users, the researchers found that current users do indeed have more coitus to orgasm, orgasms via masturbation, total orgasms, and total morning erections as well as more total sexual thoughts than past users and non-users. *However*, for the orgasmic life to be maintained, the user *must* remain on drugs. The abstainers had many more orgasms, especially coitus to orgasm, than did former users. Thus, one's sex life and athletic performance may improve while one is on steroids, but this improvement will last only as long as one is on the drugs. Once a steroid user goes off drugs, his performance will never be as good as it would have been if drugs had never been used in the first place.

Behavioral Advantages

While the drug approach has disadvantages, the behavioral approach has several lifetime advantages. First, there are behavioral ways to increase one's level of naturally occurring androgens. Having sex, cheering for a winning team "visualizing" victory in athletic performance, winning an athletic competition, and increasing one's assertiveness or aggression will all increase testosterone blood levels. Working out, eating, drinking, and resting properly—the behavioral approach—while requiring more effort than taking drugs will not only improve performance and appearance but are the very things that doctors, psychologists, trainers, and coaches recommend to improve performance and enjoyment in *all areas of one's life*. Compared to the drug approach, with dangerous side effects, the behavioral approach to improved athletic performance and physical appearance has only life-enhancing effects.

Although, for example, winners of martial arts competitions have higher levels of testosterone than do losers, poor athletic performance is not due to a "testosterone imbalance" that requires drugs. Should all nonathletic persons be given steroids because they have a "physical competition victory deficiency disorder"? Changed behaviors, improved training, and competition techniques result in improved performance and higher levels of testosterone. Just because a chemical level is associated with a problem does not mean that an "imbalance" caused the problem (psychology students will recognize this as an example of the "correlation does not imply causality" fallacy). Just as there are effective nondrug, side effect-free behavioral methods to improve performance and increase testosterone levels, there also are effective, nondrug, side effect-free, life-enhancing ways to overcome other behavioral problems.

THE BEHAVIORAL PHILOSOPHY

Rather than positing that problem behaviors are due to chemical imbalances and mental or brain dysfunction, the behavioral approach holds that problem behaviors are the result of problematic behavior-environment associations and dysfunctional reinforcement contingencies. To the average individual it may appear that problematic thoughts and feelings cause maladaptive behavior. Since thoughts and feelings appear to be "mental," "inside the person," it also may appear logical that the most effective way to change thoughts and feelings is to go "inside the person" with drugs.

The behavioral approach recognizes this appearance as an illusion. Thinking and feeling are things people *do*. Thinking and feeling are *behaviors*. Thus thinking and feeling, although sometimes scientifically difficult to "get at," are nonetheless caused by the interactions between the person and the environment. As behavior, what we think and what we feel are the results of behavior-environment associations and reinforcement contingencies. But the illusion that thinking and feeling are *initial causes* of behavior is strong. We feel something and react, and we behave. We think something, and we then do something as a result. However, as indicated by the first meanings of the very word "feel," no feelings would be possible without interactions with the causal environment. A child is first taught to feel the water, the ball, the clay, the wind, what pointed, sharp things feel like, what dull things feel like. Only later and only *after* the child is taught about feeling *overtly* things in the world that can easily be reinforced and if necessary corrected ("no, a pen feels sharp, a ball feels dull and round") can a child be taught to describe internal states as feelings too ("Honey, is the pain you are feeling inside sharp or dull?"). We must have some interaction with the environment that we "feel" before we can communicate "feelings inside." Only after an environmental interaction can we "feel," and only then can we do something overtly as a result of that interaction.

Likewise, we have some interaction with the environment that causes us to think and do something overtly as a result of that interaction. We are given a problem (environmental interaction), we think about it, and then we produce a solution (behavior). Someone insults us (environmental interaction), we feel bad, and then we cry (behavior). The feeling, thinking, and overt behaviors are all a product of one's current and historical interactions with the environment, including one's social environment. As Skinner, and before him the Russian scientist Sechenov, noted, no thinking, "cognition," or feeling would be possible without an environment with which to interact. Skinner argued, "We cannot account for the behavior of any system [including humans with problematic thoughts and feelings] while staying wholly inside it; eventually we must turn to the forces operating upon the organism [person] from without" (1953, p. 35). The causes of behavior, thoughts, and feelings "lie outside the organism, in its immediate environment and in its environmental history" (1953, p. 31). Similarly, Sechenov argued:

> It is generally accepted that if one act follows another, the two acts stand in causal relationship (post hoc—ergo propter hoc); this is why thought is generally believed to be the cause of behavior: and when the external sensory stimulus remains unnoticed...thought is even accepted as the initial cause of behavior. Add to this the extremely subjective character of thought, and you will understand how firmly man must believe in the voice of self-consciousness....In reality, however, this voice tells him the greatest of falsehoods: the initial cause of all behavior always lies, not in thought, but in external sensory stimulation, without which no thought is possible. (Sechenov, 1863 [quoted from Rachlin, 1991])

Because thoughts, feelings, and covert and overt behaviors are *all products of behavior-environment interactions*, the behavioral approach to helping problematic, dysfunctional, distressing behaviors, including feeling and thinking, is to alter the behavior-environment interactions. If distressful behaviors are due to certain problematic environmental associations, then the approach would be to extinguish, or disassociate, the problematic association(s) and replace them with appropriate, functional associations and behavior. For example, if someone has an extreme fear of public speaking, rather than be drugged before speaking, which would just hide the problem, the behavioral approach would be to extinguish the fear by having the person engage in learned relaxation techniques while speaking initially one to one and then to gradually larger warm and supportive audiences. This process of changing behavior-environment interactions removes or reduces the feeling of fear and shapes effective public speaking behaviors.

If the distressful behaviors are due to dysfunctional reinforcement contingencies, then attempts are made to develop new, functional, prosocial reinforcement contingencies. For example, a person diagnosed as "depressed" both "feels" and *acts,* or behaves, depressed. If an individual did not act depressed then the individual would not feel depressed. Both the feeling of depression and behaving depressed are a result of the person's environmental interactions. The person's family likely inadvertently reinforces depressive statements and actions, and the person likely has few nondepressive behavioral repertories that produce reinforcement (Flora, 2004). Thus the behavioral approach would be to teach the individual new behaviors that produce reinforcement and are antagonistic to feeling depressed, such as regular exercise and social skills. Once the person's behaviors are no longer "de-pressed," no longer pressed down, the individual finds that the "feelings" of depression are gone as well (there is no longer anything that is "de- pressed" to "feel"). Furthermore, because family members often unintentionally reinforce and thus maintain dysfunctional behaviors, they often must learn new ways of interaction and communication with their loved ones in order to relieve depression.

Because behavior is a product of environment interactions, and the most powerful behavioral factors in the environment are social factors, in addition to direct individual behavioral treatment of problematic behaviors, the behavioral approach also includes working with individual's families, behavioral parent training (the most effective approach for treating conduct problems), behavioral couples therapy (one of the most important elements in successful substance abuse treatment in addition to being the most effective relationship therapy), and interpersonal psychotherapy. The behavioral approach holds, and research consistently finds, that when distressful, dysfunctional behaviors are replaced with successful, functional behaviors, distressful and dysfunctional feelings and thoughts are replaced with successful, functional feelings and thoughts. The most direct way to change feelings and thoughts is not with drugs but with behavioral change.

CRITICISMS OF THE BEHAVIORAL APPROACH

The behavioral approach is not widely used because in the "mental health profession" and in society at large several pervasive myths and inaccurate criticisms exist concerning this approach. One such criticism is that the behavioral approach "ignores what goes on inside the person," ignores a person's thoughts and feelings. But the behavioral approach simply views thoughts and feelings *as behaviors* themselves rather than as causes of behaviors. When people learn to behave well, they find they "feel" well too. Indeed, the behavioral approach does not put people "on the couch" and to talk about their problems, thoughts, and feelings for an hour each week or month for years on end. This approach is ineffective. If it was effective, it would not go on for years on end (Wolpe, 1981). The behavioral approach gets the person *off the couch, doing things* that improve behavior, health, thoughts, and feelings. Furthermore, behavioral therapists are actually rated as being more empathetic and supportive toward their clients and patients than are practitioners of other "therapeutic" approaches (Greenwald, Kornblith, Hersen, Bellack, & Himmelhoch, 1981; Sloan, Staples, Cristol, Yorkston, & Whipple, 1975). Behavior therapists know that a warm, empathetic, supportive, *reinforcing* therapeutic environment is critical in getting clients to perform such important behavioral tasks as self-monitoring and behavioral homework assignments that are ultimately responsible for improved behavior, thoughts, and feelings outside of the therapist's office in the client's actual life.

The behavioral approach is criticized as "treating people like pets." It would be great if some people treated their coworkers and children as well and with as much understanding and warmth as they treated their pets. But, more seriously, both pets and people *do* respond best to consistent but warm and reinforcing interactions and environments. However, this criticism is usually meant to imply that the behavioral approach is controlling and limits individual freedoms. The truth is, the behavioral approach simply acknowledges the reality that the environment (environmental reinforcers) ultimately controls one's behavior. Once the controlling power of reinforcement is recognized, reinforcement can be, and is, used to increase individual freedom and "self-control."

For example, before behavioral reinforcement procedures were widely used with individuals suffering from severe or profound mental retardation, those individuals were frequently medically sedated and warehoused—living zombies waiting to die. But once systematic reinforcement programs began to be utilized, these individuals could be taught many important skills, independent eating, dressing, and hygiene behaviors, and vocational and recreational behaviors of which they were previously thought to be incapable. Consequently, their freedoms increased—now that they could dress themselves, they could decide what to wear; now that they could feed themselves, they could choose what to eat and how much to eat. Learned through systematic reinforcement procedures, their new recreational and vocational behaviors increased their range of possible behaviors, and increased their freedom.

The more one learns to do, the more one is free to do. Juvenile delinquents from socially, academically, and economically impoverished environments are not free to do much other than get a minimum wage job, stare at the TV, or deal drugs. But behavioral reinforcement programs can be used to teach social, academic, and vocational behaviors, and with each new skill learned the juvenile's potential behavioral freedom increases. Drugging people certainly does not increase their freedom.

"Persons who are plagued by psychiatric symptoms and who lack social skills soon find they are missing a supportive social network," argues Patrick Corrigan of the University of Chicago, but "behavior therapy actually empowers persons with severe mental illness" (Corrigan, 1997, p. 46). Corrigan argues that behavioral therapy generally, and token economies (tokens are earned for specific appropriate behaviors and exchanged for other reinforcers) specifically,

> provide a safe and structured milieu for individuals to consider their options. Research has clearly shown that the rate of chaos and aggression decreases significantly.... Second, token economies facilitate empowerment by clarifying options that a person may consider in a particular environment. Social exchange theorists argue that all interpersonal interactions are governed by exchange of rewards and punishers. However, rules governing this exchange are frequently subtle such that persons with social cognitive deficits are likely to miss them. Token economies make explicit the contingencies in a social exchange. (p. 52)

Token economies and behavioral therapy increase freedom. Furthermore, Corrigan shows that behavioral therapy teaches skills that help individuals "live independently and improve their quality of life" (p. 53). "Once again, behavior therapy has provided a technology that can help persons to overcome their cognitive deficits so that they are better able to address their day-to-day decisions" (p. 54). Finally, Corrigan concludes that behavioral therapy increases self-control:

> Persons with severe mental illness are taught to self-monitor their behavior, the situations in which these behaviors occur, and the consequences that follow. Targets of self-monitoring

may include observable behaviors like conversing with a friend, as well as internal states like feeling anxious about this situation.... Persons are then taught to reward themselves for meeting [behavioral] criteria.... Self-control techniques have been used successfully to help persons with severe mental illness, especially those with depressive disorders.... [Resulting in] more independent decision making and greater personal empowerment. (p. 55)

Drugs cannot do that.

Behavioral approaches in general, and reinforcement procedures specifically, also are falsely said to be controlling and to "undermine intrinsic interest." Neither are true. A "meta-analysis" (statistical review) conducted by Canadian researchers of *all* the studies on reward and interest found that "Rewards can be used effectively to enhance interest without disrupting performance.... Rewards can be arranged to shape performance progressively, to establish interest in activities that lack initial interest, and to maintain or enhance effort and persistence at a task" (Cameron, Banko, & Pierce, 2001, p. 27). My own research consistently finds that reinforcing reading or schoolwork by children increases the children's interest and improves performance (Flora & Flora, 1999; Flora & Poponak, 2004).

Ironically, and incorrectly, when behavior modification was just in its infancy it was harshly criticized in the article "Current Behavior Modification in the Classroom: Be Still, Be Quiet, Be Docile" (Winett & Winkler, 1972), which claimed that behavior modification did nothing but keep children still, quiet, and docile. This was strange, because in the very same issue of the *Journal of Applied Behavior Analysis*, in which the Winett and Winkler article appeared, there was an article showing how "sequential reinforcement contingencies" in a token economy improved composition-writing skills (Brigham, Graubard, & Stans, 1972). Another article in the same issue showed how "anxiety-depression" was successfully treated with the behavioral procedures of positive reinforcement and response cost (Reisinger, 1972). Additionally, in previous issues, the journal had reported on successful behavioral programs such as Achievement Place, where behavioral programs empower predelinquent boys with social and academic skills (Phillips, Phillips, Fixsen, & Wolf, 1971).

To be sure, reinforcement can be used to keep children still, quiet, and docile, but the criticism that behavioral approaches are used *just* to keep children still, quiet, and docile is especially ironic in the current situation. It is ironic because it is the drug approach that has the goal of making *all children* still, quiet, and docile! Behavioral approaches can shape quiet behavior, academic behavior, social behavior, or rowdy behavior, depending on what is appropriate for the time and place. But drugs cannot; drugs just drug. That is all they do. Drugs do not teach. Drugs drug independently of time, place, and context. Drugs such as Ritalin and Adderall are being used to do nothing but keep children still, quiet, and docile, producing a nation of zombies. But there are alternatives. The effective alternative is the behavioral approach.

Chapter 3

Eating Disorders
Anorexia, Bulimia, Binge Eating, and Obesity

Eating problems are behavioral problems. Eating is something we do. Eating is behavior. Eating disorders are behavioral disorders, not brain or chemical disorders. Of course, when eating has been out of balance for an extended length of time, chemical changes do occur. But chemical imbalances and changed brain functioning are effects, not causes, of problematic eating behaviors. As with other behaviors, both adaptive and maladaptive, the causes of problematic eating behaviors lie outside of the individual, in the individual's societal, social, and family environments, with faulty environmental associations and reinforcement contingencies.

Anorexia nervosa is a *behavioral* problem of highly restricted food intake, self-starvation, a preoccupation with thinness, and brutal overexercise. *Bulimia nervosa* is a *behaviorial problem* of excessive eating— binges, followed by purging, usually vomiting or laxative abuse. *Binge eating disorder* is a *behaviorial problem* characterized by binges without purging. The causes and complications of bulimia and anorexia are often similar, while binge eating and obesity share commonalities.

CAUSES, CONSEQUENCES, AND COMPLICATIONS OF ANOREXIA AND BULIMIA

Almost all cases (over 90%) of anorexia and bulimia are young, white women and girls of upper socioeconomic status from a highly competitive environment. These eating disorders are culturally specific; they are

29

virtually nonexistent in non-Westernized countries and are only seen when these countries start to become "Americanized." Bulimia may be the most common behaviorial problem on college campuses. In some sorority houses and women's dorms, group binge parties occur, often followed by purging. Most males with eating disorders are homosexuals and face peer pressure to be thin (Carlat, Camargo, & Herzog, 1997).

Depression often follows the development of eating disorders. Stomach acids in the mouth, the result of vomiting, cause erosion of dental enamel. "Chipmunk cheeks," swollen cheeks, result from damaged and enlarged salivary glands. Sphincter valves may become permanently eroded and damaged, making food retention impossible without surgery. Electrolyte and fluid imbalances result in heart and kidney complications that may be fatal. Death is the most serious complication of eating disorders. As many as 20% of people suffering from an eating disorder die from it or from complications of it (see Barlow & Durand, 1999, for a review of statistics).

Nothing in the brain "causes" eating disorders, but the pressure placed on women by Western-Anglo society to be thin and competitive does influence many young females to attempt to lose weight, which is the first step toward eating disorders. From being invited to a school dance, to marrying successful men, to being hired or promoted on the job, it may not be fair but it is a reality that for white Western females, more reinforcers are available to the thin than the obese. This reality causes the dieting that for some women eventually results in disordered eating behaviors and sometimes death.

Compared to white girls, black American girls, on average, have virtually no risk of developing an eating disorder. Are white Americans willing to say that white girls have a "brain disorder" requiring drug treatment that black girls do not have? Or will society admit that, on average sociocultural environmental differences account for these differences? If sociocultural environmental differences account for the differences in the rates of eating disorders (they do), then changing the sociocultural expectations that white girls face can reduce and prevent many eating disorders.

As songs such as *Brick House* by the Commodores and *Baby Got Back* by Sir Mix-a-Lot can attest, shapely, full-figured women have always been celebrated and viewed as being sexually desirable in black American culture. Consequently, black women have much healthier body self-images compared to whites. Conversely, white Western females often equate thinness with self-worth. Ironically, studies (e.g., Fallon and

Rozin, 1985) have shown that undergraduate men (presumably the vast majority were white) rated women's ideal weight higher than women think men would ideally like them to weigh—white guys apparently do like curves. White girls have been known to compare their body size to anorexic models in the media, or to themselves before they have reached their natural, post-puberty shape. The more TV that girls watch, and therefore the more exposure to thin actors and models, the more likely they will develop eating problems.

Initial weight loss usually is reinforced. The teasing stops, compliments start, and flattering social attention and invitations are received. Before the weight loss becomes excessive, the dieter may feel better and actually be healthier, allowing increased activity that results in further reinforcements. These are largely environmental reinforcers for weight loss—not brain chemistry requiring drugs. For example, during a class discussion on a different topic, one of my students volunteered that she could not floss her teeth because of extensive dental work she had had. After class she confided that her dental problems were a consequence of past purging problems that destroyed her tooth enamel. As a child she was always overweight. In 10th grade she caught mononucleosis, which resulted in a 15-pound weight loss. When she returned to school, people who had previously teased her began to compliment her on her weight loss and looks. Consequently, she attempted to diet and lose more weight. Further reinforcing her weight loss efforts, her brother's friends began to ask her on dates. When she could no longer lose weight by diet alone, she began to purge by vomiting and abusing laxatives. This continued until she was hospitalized as a result of complications from these unhealthy behaviorial patterns.

ACTIVITY ANOREXIA

In addition to restricted eating, many dieters also engage in brutal exercise regimens and often exercise for several hours a day. (My student would wake at 4 a.m. to exercise for several hours before school.) This combination of *behaviors*, food restriction plus excessive exercise, often produces *activity anorexia*. If rats are put on a restricted diet, one meal for one hour a day, they initially will lose weight. But soon they will learn to adjust, eating one very large meal, and their weight will stabilize. But if they have access to a running wheel, even though they do not have to run at all, the rats will start to run more and more, up to 10 kilometers a day, and they will eat less and less. If the running wheel is not removed and the rats are not given a less restrictive diet, then they will "voluntarily" exercise and starve themselves to death.

The reasons for this seemingly maladaptive behaviorial pattern are not completely understood, but it is believed that increased activity during periods of food shortages may be an evolutionary behavioral adaptation. Activity that otherwise would be excessive may increase the probability that an organism could find a new food source that a less active organism could not reach. Therefore, during periods of food shortages, organisms that became more active would be more "fit" in terms of natural selection. Thus organisms possessing the variation of increased activity would tend to be selected over successive generations.

It is believed that endogenous endorphin, natural brain opiates, will partly reinforce this activity—the "runner's high." That is, once significant weight loss has occurred, excessive exercise, particularly aerobic-type exercise, "feels good." Just as the heroin addict needs his or her fix of extrinsic opiates to feel good, the activity aneroxie needs excessive exercise and the consequential endogenous opiates to feel good. In sum, with activity anorexia, initial dieting and exercising occasioned and reinforced by societal factors may in part become intrinsically controlled endogenous opiates (see Pierce & Epling, 1994, for a review of activity anorexia).

BINGING AND PURGING

Of course, not all dieters and exercisers develop activity anorexia. It is a natural biological process that when food intake is restricted, discomfort occurs and craving for food becomes great, resulting in the reinforcing behavior of eating. Eating, particularly high carbohydrate foods, is pleasurable, anxiety reducing, and produces a release of endorphins, natural brain opiates. But for the dieter, this great pleasure is followed by equal or greater guilt, tension, and a sense of failure. Thus as the bulimic binges, although the activity is pleasurable, anxiety and guilt increase with each mouthful. Purging, particularly vomiting, produces immediate relief from this guilt and thus reinforces the binge-purge cycle.

Unfortunately, the person with problematic eating behaviors has learned, maybe even during infancy (see the section "Binge Eating Disorder and Obesity" that follows), that binging feels good and produces "relief" (albeit temporary), regardless of the source of stress.

Binging offers relief not only from food restriction but from a relationship breakup or job or academic setback. Binging even provides relief from a lonely afternoon. However, for many Western white girls, the very binge that produces immediate relief and reinforcement simultaneously signals failure and the loss of ultimately more important social reinforcers that are only available to the thin—fat equals failure, while thin equals fun. Thus purging is seen as a way to have one's cake and eat it too. This pattern of behavior is not without aversive health and social consequences, but it is a pattern of *behavior*, produced by behaviorial-environmental interactions and consequences, not by faulty brain chemistry. One consequence of this pattern of behavior is imbalanced body chemistry. As we will see, the best way to restore balance is to achieve equilibrum in one's life, not by constant drug use, but by changing one's life circumstances and behavior.

BINGE EATING DISORDER AND OBESITY

Many people binge on food occasionally, but not all of them have binge eating disorder (BED), and not all obese people binge. Eating a large bowl of ice cream is not really binging, nor is eating the second bowl, but eating the entire half-gallon carton is a binge, and frequently eating such large amounts in one sitting is *behavior that is out of balance*, not out-of-balance brain chemistry.

The behavior of eating is reinforced by the food that is eaten. Eating is reinforced by the smell, texture, taste, and other properties of food. There is growing evidence that eating, particularly high-fat foods and foods high in carbohydrates, results in increased dopamine and endorphin activity in the brain. Food is the universal reinforcer. From undergraduate psychology laboratories shaping a rat's bar-pressing behavior to teaching language to autistic children, food is the most frequent reinforcer for virtually limitless numbers of organisms and behaviors. Many families also teach, albeit usually unintentionally, that food produces comfort, and thus they excessively associate it with social warmth, affection, and security.

It is fine to give a child a sweet treat and kisses following a substantial physical injury or to comfort a child who has been harshly teased by older children or has suffered some other substantial defeat. However, if sweets are always used to calm a child and are associated with soothing a child *excessively*, *frequently*, and *out of proportion* to other means of comfort (hugs, play time, reading, walks, or talking and listening), then eating will become differentially associated with comfort. The child will learn that comfort is only a binge away. Binging occurs because binging, or excessive eating, has been taught. An individual binges because she or he has learned that binging is reinforcing. Binging feels good not only after a period of food restriction but anytime there is discomfort or unhappiness. This is not a brain dysfunction but a behavioral dysfunction. It is a dysfunction because binging is relied on as a method of stress reduction at the expense of more appropriate, and ultimately more effective, behavioral means of stress reduction. People with BED binge because they are unhappy. At the expense of potential long term happiness, binging provides an immediate but only a fleeting, escape from unhappiness. The proof is that these people continue to binge but remain unhappy.

BEHAVIORAL PERSPECTIVE SUMMARY

Like other behaviors, problematic eating behaviors are caused by problematic environmental reinforcement contingencies. Western society values thinness, not obesity. With anorexia, initial weight loss frequently produces copious social reinforcement. Further weight loss may produce further social reinforcement—to a point. But at that point, for many the process of activity anorexia may take over. With bulimia, success in initial weight loss varies, as does social reinforcement for weight loss. Food restriction is aversive, but weight gain is unacceptable, lest more social reinforcers become lost or forever out of reach. Binging followed by purging thus becomes a way to get relief from dieting, or other aversive situations, without socially perceived and personally unacceptable weight gain. Binging is maintained by negative reinforcement. It produces relief from life's difficulties, whether food restriction or otherwise. Purging also is maintained by negative reinforcement. It gets rid of the food and guilt of binging.

DRUG APPROACH

The drug perspective maintains that problematic eating behavior occurs because there is some sort of mysterious chemical imbalance (in Westernized white girls only) that causes the brain to malfunction and that in turn results in eating problems. Of course, there are biological-based *tendencies* for some individuals to be heavier or lighter, to eat more or less, and to be more or less active than other individuals. But "tendency" or even "predisposition" does not equal "cause," and most people with these tendencies maintain normal eating behaviors. There is no evidence for the drug approach's viewpoint, that chemical imbalances result in problematic eating behaviors.

TREATMENTS FOR PROBLEMATIC EATING BEHAVIORS

Sadly, the current state of treatment for eating disorders, like other problematic behavioral patterns, is a disservice—if not simply unethical—to those suffering from the problematic behaviors. In the early 1990s a team of researchers from Harvard University, Massachusetts General Hospital, Brown University, and UCLA conducted an extensive study, "The Current Status of Treatment for Anorexia Nervosa and Bulimia Nervosa" (Herzog, Keller, Strober, Yeh, & Pai, 1992). Their findings were disheartening, to say the least. The researchers found that "clinical decisions are not influenced primarily by treatment studies in the scientific literature [as they should be].... Several treatments [nonbehavioral "talk therapy" and drug therapy] are frequently endorsed in clinical practice despite the lack of controlled studies demonstrating their efficacy" (p. 219). Although, as we will see later, behavioral treatments are the only effective treatments for eating problems, "talking therapy is overwhelmingly endorsed for the treatment of both anorexia and bulimia nervosa... [and] there is a trend in clinical practice toward using drug therapy more frequently" (p. 215). The trend toward increased drug treatment for problematic eating behaviors has only increased, and throughout the Western world, women with eating disorders are not getting what they need—the most effective help possible. "In daily practice," writes Anita Jansen of Maastricht University, the Netherlands, "two of three psychotherapists do not treat their eating disordered patients with the best treatment available, i.e. cognitive behaviour therapy" (Jansen, 2001, p. 1007). The situation may only get worse, because as Jansen notes, "The pharmaceutical industry spends millions on the distribution of information about newly developed pills while psychologists do virtually nothing with regard to newly developed and clearly effective [behavioral] treatment protocols" (p. 1016).

Drug Treatments

In general, drug treatments "directed" at eating problems are the same brain whitewash drug treatments, primarily SSRIs and other antidepressants, directed at many other, if not most, behavioral difficulties—generalized anxiety, phobias, depression, obsessive-compulsive behavior, and post traumatic stress, to name some. How can low serotonin levels, or other monoamine levels, cause one thing in one person, such as a spider phobia, and something very different in someone else, such as binge-purge behavior? The same flu virus will cause the same flu with the same, or highly similar, symptoms in everyone who has it. The chemical hypothesis behind eating difficulties is just as absurd as the drug treatments for eating difficulties are ineffective. Problematic behaviors are caused by problematic relationships between behavior and the environment (including the social environment).

Anorexia Drug Treatment

With regard to anorexia, researchers have consistently found that "to date, no medication has been shown to change eating behavior reliably, assist weight gain, or modify its fear, or alter body image disturbance" (Johnson, Tosh, & Varnado, 1996, p. 457). More directly, *Abnormal Psychology* textbook authors Barlow and Durand simply state: "At present, drug treatments have not been found to be effective in the treatment of anorexia nervosa" (1999, p. 243). British researcher Chris Freeman agrees: "Although drugs have been widely used in the treatment of anorexia nervosa there is no convincing evidence of their efficacy" (1998, p. 72). Drugs are no more effective than placebo treatment (Attia, Haimon, Walsh, & Flater, 1998). Indeed, in a book published by the American Psychological Association (APA), *Combined Treatments for Mental Disorders* (2001), anorexia is salient by its omission in the eating disorders chapter, "Pharmacological and Psychological Treatments of Obesity and Binge Eating Disorder" (Grilo, 2001). The APA is pushing the government to pass laws allowing members of its guild, psychologists, who have very little medical training, to prescribe drugs. The book on combined treatments is apparently part of this push. Because psychologists want to prescribe drugs, and drugs have no effect on anorexia, one must ask: Are psychologists now pretending that "mental disorders" not altered by drug "treatment" do not exist? Surely such a book should discuss anorexia.

Bulimia Drug Treatment

Bulimics binge and purge as a temporary means to feel good or at least momentarily less unhappy. People that binge and purge are unhappy, therefore, it is not surprising that antidepressants (tricylic antidepressants, MAO inhibitors, and most often our close friends the SSRIs) are used in drug-based attempts to "cure" bulimia. Drug treatment reduces purging in only about half of the women who are able to tolerate the drugs, but almost as many (43% in one study, see Mitchell, Pyle, Eckert, Hatsukumi, & Zimmerman, 1990) quit treatment because of the numerous side effects. To the extent that the drugs "work" in making people "feel better," for those who can tolerate the side effects, drugs may temporally decrease binge-purge behavior. But as soon as the drugs are stopped this behavior returns. Relapse rates approach 80% for drug therapy (Johnson, Tosh, & Varnado, 1996). Another way to phrase that is that unless people *always* remain drugged, *drugs do not work* or "cure" the eating disorder. Drugs do nothing to change one's interactions with the environment. Behavior-environment contingencies are the cause of problematic behaviors. To change problematic behaviors one's behavior-environment relationships must change.

BEHAVIORAL TREATMENTS FOR EATING DISORDERS

Anorexia

Western society reinforces thinness in women. The diet industry is a multibillion-dollar industry. It is admittedly difficult to overcome these seemingly overwhelming forces in helping a person overcome anorexia. Nevertheless, with systematic behavioral contingencies, help is possible (certainly to a much greater extent than with drugs). According to Mississippi Medical Center researchers, "Data have demonstrated the efficacy of various behavioral interventions" for anorexia (Johnson et al., 1996, p. 468).

Unfortunately, help is not sought for, or by, many people with anorexia until some sort of health emergency occurs. Often the person is literally in a state of starvation. therefore, immediate weight gain is the most critical initial treatment goal. But the female with anorexia refuses to eat despite her state of starvation. Since societal, social, and family contingencies significantly contribute to the development of anorexia, establishing new social contingencies and family interactions can go a long way toward ameliorating anorexia.

Often patients and family are given a *behavioral contract* or *contingency contract* that outlines eating, exercising, and weight gain contingencies necessary for access to various reinforcing activities. Typically the patient may progress through several levels of increasing reinforcement access and decreasing supervision contingent on progressive eating, weight gain, and appropriate, nonexcessive exercise. For example, in a firm and caring but nonpunitive environment, initially the patient may be required to eat several snacks and 100% of three meals (but is also allowed to exclude three aversive foods each meal), or to substitute a nutrition shake for a meal each day in order to earn phone and TV privileges. In other words, as social reinforcement for weight loss may have been a contributing factor in the onset of weight loss and anorexia, social reinforcement for eating and weight gain is an initial factor in the treatment of anorexia.

Once patients are eating regularly and weight gain is approximately 85% to 90% of their ideal body weight, they are likely to be discharged. To maintain the healthy eating patterns started in the hospital or to develop healthy eating and exercising patterns for anorexics not hospitalized, family-oriented behavioral therapy usually is necessary. Initially, parents or significant others take charge of eating routines. Behavioral contracts that call for and provide reinforcement contingent on healthy eating and weight gain are likely to be utilized. For example, a young girl with anorexia who loves horses may be allowed to ride and groom her horse only as long as she maintains a healthy weight and eating patterns. High school or college students may be allowed to participate in gymnastics, dance, cheerleading, sorority activities, or whatever activities they find reinforcing only as long as they maintain healthy weight and eating patterns. In addition to direct educational efforts about health, exercise, body weight, starvation, healthy eating, and other factors relevant to anorexia, the behavioral contingencies implicitly teach the individual that reinforcing activities are only possible for healthy, fit people. In addition to directly encouraging healthy eating, the behavioral contingencies teach people suffering from anorexia that starving, vastly underweight people *lose* reinforcers that are available to healthy people. A starving, weak, 7-year-old girl cannot control a full-grown horse out on the trail, but a healthy, fit, well-fed 7-year-old girl can. Compared to starving, bony women, healthy, fit young women are more attractive to young men and receive more reinforcing attention from them. Dancing, cheerleading, and gymnastics are all performed better by fit, muscle-toned young women than by starving girls. Thus rather than criticize the lack of eating in a punitive manner, through positive reinforcement the behavioral approach teaches the person suffering from anorexia that a nonanorexic way of life is ultimately more reinforcing and enjoyable than is anorexia.

Once weight gain and healthy eating patterns have been well established, and sources of reinforcement incompatible with anorexia are developed, control of eating is gradually returned to the individual, and the focus of therapy may diverge to other related issues such as family dynamics and individual growth and autonomy (see, e.g., Robin, Gilroy, & Dennis, 1998).

Eating is a central feature of all human life, for without it human life would not be possible. For the vast majority of people, including those suffering from anorexia, from birth to death, eating occurs daily. Consequently, much human social activity centers around eating as well. Dinner may be the only time families come together. "Power lunches," parties, dates, weddings, and other celebrations all have food as a central feature. With society's conflicting emphasis on eating, on the one hand, and dieting, on the other, the formerly anorexic person is always at risk. A harsh comment about looks, weight, or shape may convince the formerly anorexic person to return to an unhealthy, anorexic lifestyle.

Although the former anorexic will always be confronted with society's obsession with thinness and society's reinforcement of thinness, cognitive behavior therapy (CBT) can provide effective posthospitalization treatment for anorexia and help prevent a return to anorexic eating patterns. When adult anorexic patients were given CBT posthospitalization, the relapse rate was only 22% (Pike, Walsh, Vitousck, Wilson, & Bauer, 2003), far better than drug relapse rates.

Indeed, SSRI drugs may have *no* effect. A study on SSRI drugs with malnourished, underweight anorexics with the no-nonsense title "Are Serotonin Selective Reuptake Inhibitors Effective in Underweight Anorexia Nervosa?" concluded *no*: "Results suggest that SSRI medication had no effect on clinical symptoms of malnourished underweight anorexics" (Ferguson, La Via, Crossan, & Kaye, 1999, p. 11).

Bulimia

The behavioral approach to bulimia involves education, behavior change, and gradual exposure to the cues that trigger overeating (stimuli, emotions, interpersonal interactions). First the patient learns the health consequences of the binge-purge eating pattern (from "chipmunk cheeks" and dental problems to death). Then the patient is taught to eat small, manageable meals thoughout the day to avoid the starvation, then binge, then purge pattern that is the bulimic lifestyle. Finally, the patient is gradually exposed to the triggers for binging while practicing alternative healthy behaviors, such as applied relaxation, to counter the triggers.

As binging and purging are behaviors, it is not surprising that therapy targeting these behaviors for change are effective. A review of 16 "controlled treatment outcome studies" that "represent the best evidence for the efficacy of CBT" (Anderson & Maloney, 2001, pp. 972–973) found that "CBT significantly reduces binge eating and purgative behavior," and that "data from self-report questionnaires indicates that CBT significantly reduces shape and weight concerns to normative levels" (2001, p. 983). CBT helps female patients learn what their normal shape and weight should be. It is difficult to see how taking a drug could teach that.

Not only is cognitive behavioral therapy effective, it is *lasting*. A study of "exposure with response prevention in cognitive-behavioral therapy for bulimia" (p. 127) of 113 women found that "at the 3-year follow-up, 85% of the sample had no current diagnosis of bulimia nervosa," e.g., "treatment gains are maintained after 3 years" (Carter, McIntosh, Joyce, Sullivan, & Bulik, 2003, p. 127).

CBT is effective and lasting and makes drug "treatment" completely unnecessary. The study "fluoxetine [Prozac] and fluvoxamine [Luvox] with individual cognitive-behavior therapy in binge eating disorder" found that binging was significantly reduced in the CBT only and CBT-drug combination groups but *not* in the drug-only groups. This led the authors to conclude that "CBT was more effective than FLX [Prozac] or FLV [Luvox] in the treatment of BED [binge eating disorder]" (Ricca, Mannucci, Mezzani, Moretti, DiBernardo, Bertelli, Rotella, & Faravelli, 2001, p. 298). Furthermore, adding drugging to CBT to treat eating difficulties does *not* add any effectiveness.

THE BOTTOM LINE

In the chapter "Treatments for Eating Disorders" in *A Guide to Treatments That Work* (2002), it is concluded that for bulimia:

1. CBT seems more acceptable to patients than antidepressant medication. 2. The dropout rate is lower with CBT than with pharmacological treatments. 3. CBT seems superior to treatment with a single antidepressant drug. 4. Combining CBT with antidepressant medication is significantly more effective than medication alone. 5. Combining CBT and antidepressant medication provides few [if any] consistent benefits over CBT alone. 6. CBT plus medication has not been shown to be superior to CBT plus a pill placebo. 7. The combination of CBT and antidepressant medication may be more effective than CBT alone in reducing anxiety and depressive symptoms [this claim is countered in the depression chapter]. 8. Longer term maintenance of change appears to be better with CBT than with antidepressant drugs. (Wilson & Fairburn, 2002, p. 565)

Given these conclusions, that using drugs is the *least* effective treatment method, the *only* overall conclusion is that it is unethical to offer drugs instead of providing effective behavioral therapies (CBT, exposure with response prevention) in the treatment of dangerous eating patterns.

Chapter 4

Specific Phobias

Phobias are *irrational fears* that cause personal distress and can interfere with a person's daily functioning. For example, a person with an elevator phobia may avoid buildings with elevators. Such a phobia would limit the person's employment, living, and social possibilities, and could preclude the person from receiving important personal services. A person with an elevator phobia may refuse to visit doctors, lawyers, or government officials if getting to the office requires a trip in an elevator. In social phobia, the irrational fear is of social situations. Such a phobia, left untreated, may develop into agoraphobia. People labeled with agoraphobia often refuse to step foot outside of their houses or apartments for years.

LEARNING AND BEHAVIOR

Humans are born with a fear of falling and a fear of loud noises; *all other fears, rational and irrational, are learned.* They are learned either "vicariously" (through observation or from the verbal community through many sources—novels, religious writings, etc.), or by direct experiences. For example, a dog bite may result in a fear of dogs—a direct conditioning experience. But more common are vicarious conditioning experiences. For example, a lick in the face is the most harm my dog would ever do to a child. But in my neighborhood, when children see me walking my dog up the street, almost invariably one child will scream and start to run. The other children will respond not to my dog, but to the first child's screaming and running by doing the same. When they "safely" reach a porch, there are great dramatic expressions

43

of relief, followed by laughter. Although no child was harmed by the dog, all the children learned to fear dogs and that running away from dogs is reinforcing.

Regardless of the source of learning, vicarious or direct, *all phobic fears can be effectively treated as conditioned responses.* All behaviors that attempt to avoid the phobic situation or escape from the situation can be effectively treated as learned instrumental or operant responses maintained by reinforcement. For example, the sight of an elevator in a building may elicit conditioned fear, and leaving the building is reinforced by escaping the situation and also reinforced by a reduction in the anxiety caused by proximity to the elevator.

This analysis indicates a straightforward behavioral treatment for phobias: exposure and response prevention (ERP). In fact, ERP originally was developed for the treatment of phobias. Because the fear of the phobic object or situation is an irrational and a learned conditioned response, repeated exposure to the feared object or situation leads to extinction of the fear and anxiety. Often the person with the phobia will accept treatment only if the exposure is gradual and will progress through a "fear hierarchy." For example, a person with an elevator phobia may first be asked to just stand outside of a building that has an elevator. Once the fear in this situation has dissipated, standing in the lobby may be next, then standing next to the elevator, then standing in an elevator with the door open, then being in a elevator with the door closed, then riding up and down one level, and so on, until the individual is riding up and down elevators in skyscrapers.

The response prevention, not allowing the person to leave or escape the situation until the fear has dissipated, is critical. If the person "responds" to the situation by leaving the building that has an elevator, by running away from the dog, or whatever the situation is, then he or she will experience a reduction in fear and anxiety, not by prolonged exposure but by the escape response. Because this escape removes the person from the source of the fear and anxiety, just as purging is reinforcing for the bulimic, escape can reinforce or strengthen the phobia. Thus response prevention is as critical as exposure in effectively eliminating phobias.

ERP is *very* effective in treating phobias. Everything from common phobias such as spider phobia to more problematic anxiety "disorders," including "social anxiety disorder" (which may require additional *behavioral* components such as relaxation training and social skill training), to uncommon phobias such as "vaginal penetration phobia" (Vonk & Thyer, 1995) can effectively be treated with ERP—without drugs.

DRUGS

Despite the repeated proven effectiveness of behavioral treatment of these anxiety problems, *Abnormal Psychology* textbook author Steven Schwartz notes: "At some point, practically everyone with performance anxiety, social phobia, or any other anxiety disorder will be offered anxiolytics drugs (*lysis* is Greek for "dissolve; anxiolytics "dissolve" anxiety)" (Schwartz, 2000, p. 159). The anxiolytics are generally the benzodiazepines, including Xanax, Librium, and "mother's little helper," Valium. Schwartz also notes that like many other supposedly precise psychiatric drugs, "the precise action of the benzodiazepines is not well understood" (p. 159). But it is known that these drugs affect the neurotransmitter GABA, as does alcohol. Of course, for thousands of years we have had a widely available anti-anxiety drug—alcohol. In fact, some alcoholics love "bennies," because on these drugs they only have to drink a little to get the same effect as they normally would get from drinking a lot. Some anxious people take a drink before and during parties, while some people take "bennies," doctor prescribed, or not. Now the SSRIs (e.g., Praxil and Prozac) are being aggressively promoted for anxiety disorders, including phobic fears. *Whatever one's problem, increasing serotonin activity will cure it*! Now one can feel good about being anxious.

As with the SSRIs and other psychiatric drugs, "bennies" have many adverse side effects, including addiction, and relapse is likely when the medication is withdrawn. "Instead of learning effective ways of coping with panic-inducing situations," writes Schwartz, "habitual benzodiazepine users may come to rely on the drug to get them through, and they may panic when the drug is withdrawn" (p. 160). That is, the drugs may cause the very problem users were meant to address. Furthermore, if rebound occurs, a likely outcome, given the addictive nature of the drugs, the problem—panic, anxiety, fear—will be worse than if drugs had never been taken in the first place. Finally, Schwartz notes, "Medication, even when it temporarily relieves anxiety, does nothing to overcome helplessness or to teach new coping skills" (p. 164). This is precisely the problem with drugging behavior problems as a course of treatment. Conversely, behavioral approaches to behavioral problems directly teach people ways to overcome phobias and helplessness and to develop coping skills.

A LOGICAL COMPARISON

Exposure therapy *is* the treatment of choice for phobic fears. The report "Exposure Therapy in the Treatment of Vaginal Penetration Phobia: A Single-Case Evaluation," by researchers M. Elizabeth Vonk and Bruce A. Thyer (1995, p. 359), concurs:

> Exposure therapy is widely recognized as a treatment of choice for individuals [with] specific and social phobias. The American Psychological Association's *Task Force on Promotion and Dissemination of Psychological Procedures* has recently prepared a summary of treatments of documented efficacy, and exposure treatment for phobias is described as a "well established treatment." (Task Force, 1995, p. 23)

Vonk and Thyer found that "a specific phobia to vaginal penetration fears was effectively treated with graduated exposure involving self-conducted and partner-assisted homework exercises. Treatment produced a complete resolution of the problem within 12 sessions" (1995, p. 359). Previously, months on psychodynamic therapy had been ineffective, but by using the behavioral approach, the young woman learned how to cope with her fears, overcome her anxiety, and have pleasurable sexual intercourse.

One can ask how the drug approach would be used to overcome this phobia. Of course, as is frequently done in similar situations the historical anti-anxiety drug could be used—alcohol. The woman could be given alcohol until she passes out, or nearly passes out, artificial lubrication could perhaps be applied, and penetration then could be achieved. This scenario often happens in cases of date rape. The female also could be drugged with bennies or SSRIs and then penetrated. But if this drug approach had been taken, what would the female have learned? She would not have learned to have a satisfying sexual encounter in an intimate relationship or ways to cope with anxiety. No, she would have learned, "I can have sex if I'm drunk, or drugged out. If I'm not drunk or drugged, I'm too scared." But instead of being drugged, the behavioral approach taught her safe, nondrug relaxation and coping skills.

A DIRECT EMPIRICAL COMPARISON

Fortunately vaginal penetration phobia is rare. However, fear of the dentist and the dental office, "dental phobia," is more common. But dental fears, much like other phobias, can be eliminated with straightforward training and with a success rate that should shame those promoting the drug delusion for such problems. In a direct "comparison between one-session psychological treatment and benzodiazepine in dental phobia" (Thom, Sartory, & Johren, 2000), the inferiority of the drug approach was clearly established.

Dental patients given psychological treatment were first instructed in progressive relaxation, given information about the nature of anxiety, and then introduced to anxiety management training, "instructed that they would be able to control anxiety by actively relaxing their muscles and by slow abdominal breathing while lying in the dental chair" (p. 380), and they were given additional, brief "exposure to phobic situations and anxiety management training" (p. 380). Finally, "patients were asked to practice stress management training daily until the surgery appointment" (p. 380). In sum, patients given "psychological treatment" were taught no-nonsense information about anxiety, information about the situation they feared, and stress management and were asked to practice what they learned at home. That is, they were educated about their problem and empowered to overcome it.

Conversely, dental patients in the drug group were administered standard doses of a benzodiazepine based on body weight 30 minutes before dental treatment. Note how similar this standard drug treatment is to the behavior of the fearful person who "self-medicates" by getting drunk to reduce anxiety immediately before dental treatment. Not surprisingly, like the self-medicating person who gets drunk to reduce anxiety, patients given "bennies" did report less anxiety during dental surgery.

However, the psychological treatment produced equal initial reductions in anxiety. But that was just the start. "Phobic patients in the benzodiazepine condition showed relapse after dental treatment, whereas those in the psychological treatment condition showed further improvement until the follow-up 2 months later" (p. 378). Seventy percent of the psychological treatment patients continued dental treatment, but only 20% of the drugged patients continued treatment. Giving drugs for behavioral problems is analogous to giving a hungry person a fish, and a smelly fish at that. Empowering a person with anxiety reduction procedures and behavioral training is analogous to teaching a hungry person to fish.

When people are taught how to fish they do not need to buy fish anymore. Perhaps this is one reason the APA is waging state-by-state battles for its members, who do not attend medical school or receive medical training, to win the right to prescribe drugs for their clients. To bolster the academic and scientific credibility of this drug drive, the APA published the book *Combined Treatments for Mental Disorders: A Guide to Psychological and Pharmacological Interventions* (Sammons & Schmidt, 2001). When the evidence is weighed, including the evidence targeted to win drug prescription privileges, it is clear that behavioral approaches are more effective than drugging people. This is especially true for phobias. In fact, drugging people who have a phobia may make the situation worse.

In the APA book, the researchers writing on combining drug and psychological treatments for phobias were forced to conclude: "Cognitive-behavioral treatment, particularly exposure-based treatment, appears to be empirically justified as the treatment of choice for social phobia" (Schmidt, Koselka, & Woolaway-Bickel, 2001, p. 102) Cognitive-behavioral treatments have "better efficacy and do not possess the high relapse rates and side-effects profiles that are associated with pharmaco-therapy" (p. 102). Combining drugs with cognitive-behavioral treatment "may even lead to poorer outcomes" (p. 102). To their credit, the APA authors do acknowledge some problems of drugging patients:

> Another potential pitfall that may occur in combined treatments is the temptation for patients to overrely on medications in the context of both acute and chronic anxiety. By necessity, cognitive-behavioral interventions require that patients use skills and knowledge in the context of feared stimuli in order to learn that they can master their anxiety. Patients who routinely take medications prior to fear-provoking situations may not have the opportunity to practice cognitive-behavioral skills because of relatively low levels of anxiety. (Schmidt et al., 2001, p. 103)

The above acknowledgment shows precisely what is wrong with drugging people who have behavioral problems in general—not just phobias. The APA writers also admit that the few patients who do over-come the odds and improve with behavioral treatment combined with drugs are likely to falsely "overattribute their positive, end-state func-tioning to their medication use" (p. 103). The correct attribution of their positive end-state functioning would be to attribute the success to new behavioral skills and knowledge. Yet rather than taking an ethical stance advocating effective behavioral treatment and urging the discon-tinuation of drugging people with strong, specific, "phobic" fears, the APA guild continues to push for the legal right for its members to push drugs for profit.

In contrast, in *A Guide to Treatments that Work*, researchers writing on "pharmacological treatments for anxiety disorders" make the nonbi-ased conclusion that "pharmacological treatments have not proven effec-tive for specific phobias. In fact, use of benzodiazepines may reduce therapeutic effects of exposure treatment" (Roy-Byrne & Cowley, 2002, p. 349). *A Guide to Treatments that Work* is published by Oxford University Press, not by a guild fighting to increase the profits of its members with prescription privileges—the APA. Therefore, conclusions reached in the "guide" are more likely to be data driven rather than profit driven. Behavior therapy empowers people to overcome their fears. Drugging people only gives them a chemical blanket to avoid and hide from their fears.

SOCIAL PHOBIA

Social phobia is a specific, relatively common problem in which one suf-fers from "extreme, enduring, irrational fear and avoidance of social or performance situations" (Barlow & Durand, 1999, p. G-19). The December 17, 2000, *Parade* magazine proclaimed on its cover that "Ten million Americans, including these stars, have suffered from some form of social phobia, a dread of human contact that can be paralyzing. DO YOU SHARE THEIR FEAR?" The smiling stars who claimed to have social phobia included Cher, Donald Sutherland, Carly Simon, Joan Baez, Barbra Streisand, Renee Fleming, and Donny Osmond. If it is true that these stars, these "*social* lites," who have performed in front of mil-lions of fans, really have social phobia, then it clearly shows that the problem can be effectively dealt with, and that social anxiety is a normal and sometimes *helpful* thing to have (If you want to be a star, maybe "social phobia" is a good thing!). Clearly this "dread" has not stopped these celebrities from human contact, socializing, stardom, or becoming millionaires as a result of their social skills, their *social behaviors.*

A common finding in psychological research is the "Yerkes-Dodson law" that shows that performance improves as arousal increases—up to a point. After maximal performance is reached, further increases in arousal decrease performance (an "inverted U"-shaped curve). Thus to perform well in social situations—in the classroom, in a meeting, at a party, or on stage—some arousal, some anxiety, is necessary. Only when this arousal becomes too great does it result in behavioral problems and reduced performance.

Historically, this overarousal, this social anxiety, has been dealt with by "self-medication." The *Parade* article claims that 75% of people with social phobia become alcoholics (Meyer, 2000). The saga of the star who loses it all to alcohol and other drugs is well known. At least some of this drug abuse is attributable to self-attempts to control social or performance anxiety. However, social phobia is a *behaviorial* problem and like other behaviorial problems, it is most effectively dealt with by behavioral methods.

Nevertheless, with social phobia the drug companies have another opportunity to push their products, and they are doing just that. Not surprisingly the drugs of choice are the all-purpose, chemical, whitewash drugs, the SSRIs. With the help of some pediatricians, the drug companies are even pushing these drugs on children who are simply shy within normal ranges. A concerned aunt wrote to the pharmacist and nutritionist team Joe and Teresa Graedon about this issue asking, "Is Paxil [an SSRI] safe for a child?" The Graedons' answer should be taken to heart.

> Paxil is approved by the Food and Drug Administration for *adults* with extreme shyness (social phobia or social anxiety disorder). In one study, *two-thirds* of those treated responded well. Treating young children with such drugs is controversial. Antidepressants such as Paxil, Prozac, and Zoloft can cause nausea, constipation, dry mouth, anxiety, tremor, and insomnia. *Researchers have not determined if they are safe for long-term use in shy children.* Your niece might benefit from behavioral treatment. "Social effectiveness therapy" has been shown to help up to *three-fourths* of shy children to learn social skills and adapt better to groups. Such an approach might be worth considering before embarking on a drug program. (Graedon & Graedon, 2000b, italics added).

"Worth considering" indeed. What would a drug program teach? If one is feeling anxious, take drugs! Is this what we want to teach our children? Furthermore, two thirds (66%) is not as effective as three fourths (75%). These same results hold true for adults as well as children.

THE BEHAVIORAL APPROACH

In his review of treatments for anxiety disorders, medical researcher James Ballenger summarizes the behavioral treatment for social phobia:

> As with PD [panic disorder], the psychological treatment of SP [social phobia] shown to be effective is CBT (which involves exposure), cognitive restructuring, and, in some cases, social skills training. Exposure involves a confrontation with the feared situation in real life (in vivo), in imagination, or in role-playing situations in therapy. Combined exposure and CBT has been most successful, particularly in a group setting (CBGT) supplemented by in vivo (homework) exposures. (Ballenger, 1999, p. 1582)

When given this type of behavioral treatment, improvement was 81% maintained at 5 1/2 years later! Drugs cannot match this. They do not teach social skills or rational thinking skills (via cognitive restructuring). Drugs teach people to take drugs and, if they do not want to relapse, to keep taking drugs. Indeed, Ballenger notes, "In most studies, relapse after discontinuation of medication has been relatively high, ranging from one third to three fourths of patients." But with behavioral treatment, "maintenance of gains and low relapse rates were observed." For example, Richard Heimberg of the University at Albany and Michael Liebowitz of the New York State Psychiatric Institute found that phenelzine treatment for social phobia resulted in a 50% relapse after 6 months of those patients who improved, but behavioral treatment resulted in only a 17% relapse (reported in Azar, 1995). Drugs only teach people to drug, and with up to 75% relapse, most must keep right on drugging. But the behavioral approach teaches skills that are useful and productive across and throughout one's life. For example, someone taught social skills and rational thinking to deal with anxiety occasioned by business meetings can apply those same behavioral skills at parties and family reunions. Conversely, the person taught to take drugs to relieve anxiety over business meetings will only have learned to take drugs, so that is what she or he will do at parties and family reunions. Corporate profits, not helping people, are why drugs are promoted for social phobia.

When dealing with performance anxiety and social phobia, choosing behavioral treatment over drugs has benefits beyond mere reductions in anxiety that directly impact people's livelihoods. Behavioral treatment can actually improve the quality of performance. When behavioral treatment was compared to buspirone (Buspar, the most popular anti-anxiety drug) in treating the performance anxiety of professional musicians, the behavioral treatment not only produced significant reduction in anxiety but also resulted in improved quality of musical performance and improved performance confidence. Drugs did not achieve this (Clark & Stewart, 1991). That is, with behavioral treatment, the musicians became better musicians! Drugs drug, but behavioral treatment trains and teaches.

The new "miracle" drugs, the SSRIs, the brain chemical whitewash drugs (Prozac, Paxil, Zoloft , etc.), fare no better than the older, ineffective anti-anxiety drugs. British researchers recently compared behavioral exposure therapy to sertraline (an SSRI) for social phobia and included a 1-year follow-up. The results revealed that the patients in the exposure therapy group had "further improvement" during follow-up, whereas the sertraline drug group had "significant deterioration" (Haug, Blomhoff, Hellstrom, Holme, Humble, Modsbu, & Wold, 2003).

The only logical conclusion from these studies is that if one wants to overcome social fears and continue to improve after treatment, then behavioral treatment is the treatment of choice. But if one wants to hide from a problem while the problem continues to escalate, then drugs are the "treatment" of choice.

GENERALIZED ANXIETY DISORDER (GAD)

In many ways the label generalized anxiety disorder (GAD) is like the one-size-fits-all suit in the wholesale warehouse of the psychiatric and pharmaceutical industry. In other words, when there is no obvious disease with which to label an unhappy person, then labeling the person with GAD will "fit well enough." GAD also is a great "bonus buy." "In fact, studies have found GAD to be the most frequently assigned additional diagnosis for patients who meet criteria for another anxiety or mood disorder" (Barlow, Raffa, & Cohen, 2002, p. 323). "Hey, we already sold them on X, Y, and Z, let's sell them on GAD too." In short, selling the label "GAD" satisfies all parties involved.

The drug company is satisfied because now it has a new customer. With the label "GAD," another "disordered" person is supposedly in need of a whitewash SSRI drug such as Paxil (the first SSRI drug given government approval to "treat" GAD). Indeed, in a drug pamphlet targeted at potential customers, GlaxoSmithKline (2001), the makers of Paxil, claims: "For the 10 million people who suffer with GAD, ... worry is not just a part of life ... it is a *way* of life." The implication is that 10 million people, including the reader of the pamphlet, should be buying and taking this drug *as a way of life.* Talk about customer retention!

The psychiatrists or other "mental health professionals" are satisfied because by labeling the person they may believe that they have "explained" the person's unhappiness. Additionally, by recommending that the person be drugged, the professionals may believe that they have given the best "treatment" possible. Thus the professionals come off as effective treatment providers, appearing highly knowledgeable, thus their feelings of competency and self-worth are likely to increase. The professionals' financial bottom line also will improve. But their "explanation" is a pseudo-explanation—simply a label that "explains away" rather than explains the problem ("Your worry and unhappiness is because you have GAD. Take a drug. I know you have GAD because you worry and are unhappy." This is no explanation). The label "GAD" does nothing to identify or address the sources of the person's unhappiness. Furthermore, just as getting drunk may give a spouse reprieve from an unhappy marriage yet does nothing to resolve the causes behind the unhappy marriage, SSRI drug "treatment" does nothing to identify, address, or resolve the sources of worry that a GAD person may have. But identifying, addressing, and helping resolve the sources of worry of this person is exactly what the professional should be doing.

But more ironically and dishearteningly, the worried, unhappy person given the label "GAD" is likely to leave the office with a (false) feeling of satisfaction. He or she is led to believe that the source of unhappiness has been identified, that a professional "understands" what is wrong, and that effective treatment has been given ("It's a brain chemical imbalance after all, nothing to do with your situation and what you do or don't do"). All of these beliefs are wrong. The sources of unhappiness have *not* been identified. The professional does *not* understand the problem. Effective treatment has *not* been given (see text that follows). Instead, the person's brain has only been given the one-size-fits-all typical chemical whitewash (an SSRI), and if someone would help this worried person examine her or his life she or he would discover that the sources of worry and unhappiness have not yet been identified and addressed.

People who are labeled with GAD often have broad worries and may describe themselves as anxious, exhausted, tense, or overwhelmed—just as *every normal human being* appropriately feels at various times in life. For the person labeled with GAD, these feelings are persistent, and the sources may not be acknowledged. But as is the case with many other "psychological disorders," rather than the patient with a disease who needs treatment and is coming to the professional, a worried person with GAD visits a "professional" and is then given this disease or disorder label by the professional. Rather than call people who have difficulties with persistent anxiety "disordered"—which is exactly what the label "GAD" does—professionals should help them identify the life stressors responsible for the persistent anxiety and help them learn productive coping behaviors, anxiety management, and relaxation. This is part of the behavioral approach.

The Behavioral Approach to Problems of Generalized Anxiety

Highly effective, nonmysterious, straightforward treatments have been developed for the behaviors and problems associated with generalized anxiety. As is the case with other behavioral difficulties, effective behavioral treatment may require some work and effort. But the drug approach, which assumes that the problem is caused by a "brain chemical imbalance," requires no more effort than washing down a pill in the morning, a reality that makes drugs preferred by many. This is not real *treatment*, however. To mask the problem with drugs is no more than pill popping to escape from, rather than deal with, life's problems.

In *A Guide to Treatments That Work*, several behavioral approaches for GAD are identified and reviewed. In anxiety management, "the treatment components included psychoeducation about anxiety, relaxation, distraction, cognitive restructuring, and exposure [to anxiety-producing situations] through graded practice.... In addition, patients were encouraged to identify their strong points... were actively involved in their treatment by establishing goals and creating homework assignments" (Barlow et al., 2002, p. 324). This anxiety management produced "significant" improvements, and "in addition, these gains were maintained or improved at 6-month follow-up" (p. 324). Six months after taking drugs there is no "further improvement," because nothing has been taught, and no new behaviors (other than pill popping) have been learned. But when learning has occurred, when new effective behavioral skills and coping methods have been acquired, they can be applied in future situations to minimize and control anxiety.

One behavioral therapy [BT] was based on the rationale that "anxiety is maintained by avoidance of anxiety-producing situations, the person's reaction to the symptoms, and loss of confidence" (Barlow et al., 2002, p. 325). In other words, anxiety is due to *behavior*. Based on this rationale, the behavioral therapy "consisted of progressive muscle relaxation, reducing avoidance through graduated exposure [to anxiety producing situations], and building confidence by reinitiating pleasurable activities" (p. 325). In other words, the treatment consisted of teaching the patient to *change his or her behavior*. The "if... then" logic is simple: If the problem is due to behavior, then the solution is to change one's behavior. Most importantly, BT is effective: "The patients in the BT group improved significantly on all but one measure of anxiety and maintained their gains 6 months later" (2002, p. 326).

Similarly, cognitive behavioral treatment (CBT) uses the rationale that "anxiety is maintained by anxious thoughts and the lack of self-confidence, which can be controlled by recognizing anxious thoughts, *seeking* helpful alternatives, and *taking action* to test these alternatives" (Barlow et al., 2002, pp. 325–326, italics added). As with BT, the CBT consisted of teaching the patient to *change his or her behavior*. The CBT was found to produce "superior" treatment, and a second study found that at 1-year follow-up, 57.9% of CBT patients "met a high, end-state functioning criterion (meaning they were close to 'cured')" (Barlow et al., 2002, p. 326).

Comparing Effectiveness: Drugging versus Changing Behavior

First, CBT "has been shown to be superior to benzodiazepine medication in several controlled clinical trials" (Barlow et al., 2002, p. 326). Second, *drug treatment can make the situation worse*: "A recent study (Garcia, Micallef, Dubenil, Philippot, Jouve, & Blin, et al., 2000) demonstrated *increases in negative emotions* and *decreases in positive emotions* in both high- and low-anxiety volunteers given lorazepam [trade name Ativan, a benzodiazepine]" (Roy-Byrne & Cowley, 2002, p. 345, italics added). Third, effectively treating problems of generalized anxiety simply does *not* require drugs. A recent study compared behavioral anxiety management training (AMT) with a placebo or buspirone (Buspar) to nondirective therapy with a placebo or buspirone. The AMT was "designed to be *educational* and interactive: anxiety was explained, progressive relaxation *taught*, triggers and avoidance *examined, . . . homework tasks* set and the importance of *practicing skills learnt* emphasised" (Bond, Wingrove, Curran, & Lader, 2002, p. 268, italics added). The results of this study led the authors to conclude that "a short course of psychological therapy, *whether or not accompanied by active medication,* was an effective treatment for patients diagnosed as having quite severe GAD" (p. 267, italics added). Furthermore, "patients assigned to buspirone were significantly more likely to drop out of the study," presumably due to averse side effects (p. 270).

Finally, and most importantly, although Paxil is now being pushed as the "treatment" of choice for anxiety problems (e.g., GAD), comparing effects across studies clearly reveals that *Paxil is likely the least effective "therapy" of all!* A study published in the *American Journal of Psychiatry*, titled "Paroxetine [the generic name for Paxil] Treatment of Generalized Anxiety Disorder: A Double-Blind, Placebo-Controlled Study," using 566 patients, found that "remission was achieved by 30% and 36% of patients in the 20- and 40-mg paroxetine [Paxil] groups, respectively, compared with 20% given placebo" (Rickels, Zaninelli, McCafferty, Bellew, Lyenger, & Sheehan, 2003, p. 749). In other words, 64% and 70% did *not* improve, and the reported "improvement" was only 16% or 10% better than placebo. How can these poor results justify putting 10 million Americans on Paxil? Conversely, a recent study in *Behavior Research & Therapy* reported that "55% of CT [cognitive therapy] and 53.3% of AR [applied relaxation] patients recovered [from GAD] at 6-month follow-up. These results confirm that CT and AR are effective treatments for GAD" (Arntz, 2003, p. 633). Score: 30% or 36% (if you *double the dosage*) for Paxil. One also needs to discount placebo effects, or the score is 10% and 16% for Paxil, versus 55% of CT or 53% for AR! Other results for behaviorally based treatments are even stronger. As mentioned earlier, Borkovec and Costello (1993) found 57.9% of patients receiving CBT to be high end-state functioning (e.g., cured), at 1-year follow-up. Score, giving every benefit of the doubt, Paxil 36%, versus CBT 57.9%. Other than for profit, why would Paxil ever be considered?

Other studies of CBT find equally impressive long term results. In a study of group CBT patients (in-group CBT problems are discussed and skills are practiced in a group of patients rather one-on-one with a therapist), those with generalized anxiety participating in CBT "made *further gains* over the 2-year follow-up phase of the study" (Dugas, Ladouceur, Leger, Freeston, Langolis, Provercher, & Boisvert, 2003, p. 821, italics added). A CBT treatment study with "late-life generalized anxiety disorder" found that "gains for patients in CBT were maintained or *enhanced* over 1-year follow-up" (Stanely, Beck, Novy, Averill, Swanna, Diefenbach, & Hopko, 2003, p. 309, italics added). The *only* way to maintain, much more the only way to enhance, the effects of drugging people is to increase the dosage. But when people are *taught* skills, they can apply those new skills to future situations and also use them to acquire even more skills and life-enhancing activities. When it comes to the choice to drug people with generalized anxiety problems or teach them effective coping behaviors and skills to reduce or eliminate the anxiety, there is only one ethical decision.

PANIC DISORDER

We all have panicked at one time or another. We fear we have missed the bus to an important job interview or misplaced a paycheck. But we realize the reasons behind our panic, even when the panic is out of proportion to the problem—perhaps we did not miss the bus after all and the paycheck was in our shirt pocket all along. However, the person who is labeled as having a panic disorder suffers from chronic anxiety about the possibility of having an attack and *severe* panic attacks without obvious causes, attacks that seemingly come from "out of the blue." During a panic attack, the sufferers' heart rate may soar from under 70 to over 100 beats per minute and forehead muscle tension may more than double, and such people have reported that during the attack they "thought they were going to die." In short, although usually lasting no more than a few minutes, a panic attack is one of the most unpleasant experiences a person can have.

Wherever the sufferer is, and whatever the sufferer is doing at the time of the attack, the location and activity are associated with the attack and consequently are avoided by the sufferer as being "unsafe." For example, through basic conditioning, if an attack occurs in the park while one is playing ball, then parks and playing ball are associated with panic attacks, and the sufferer consequently avoids them. As generalization occurs (instead of avoiding *the* park, *all* parks are avoided), and attacks occur in new situations, the sufferer may develop *panic disorder with agoraphobia*. Thus agoraphobia, a condition that causes people to refuse to leave their houses or apartments for years, is caused by panic disorder. "All the evidence now points to the conclusion," writes *Abnormal Psychology* authors Barlow and Durand, "that agoraphobic avoidance behavior is simply one complication of severe unexpected panic attacks" (1999, p. 121).

As is the case with people who have generalized anxiety problems, those who have panic attacks have significant, unacknowledged sources of life stress. Additionally, people who have panic attacks may not have learned effective coping skills and proactive behaviors during childhood and early adulthood. In fact, they may have learned to be helpless (see the chapter on depression). Thus instead of coping and being proactive, sufferers are anxious and panic. Those with anxiety and panic attacks unintentionally have been taught to be anxious as a result of their life events and present circumstances.

Drug Treatment for Panic Disorder and Agoraphobia

Because panic attacks seem to occur out of nowhere (an external cause has not been pinpointed), and agoraphobia appears to be a generalized fear of all places, drug promoters argue that there must be an internal neurochemical cause that should be treated with drugs. But just because an external cause has not been found does not mean that there are no external causes, such as dysfunctional social and family relations and other unacknowledged life stressors. Nor does it logically follow that in the absence of an obvious external cause there must be an internal neurochemical cause.

Nevertheless, with the same disappointing results and numerous side effects, the same general brain whitewash drugs used for other behavioral problems are used for panic problems and agoraphobia. Benzodiazepines, tricyclic antidepressants, and the SSRIs are all pushed as treatments for panic and agoraphobia.

The "bennies," like their close chemical cousin, alcohol, are highly addictive. They decrease alertness and impair motor functioning. Many elderly people fall and break their hips not just because they have brittle bones but because just as being drunk impairs motor skills benzodiazepines impair their motor skills (Ray, Gurwitz, Decker, & Kennedy, 1992).

The antidepressants produce such strong side effects, including dry mouth, dizziness, and possible sexual dysfunction that many sufferers refuse to remain on the drugs (see, e.g., Barlow & Durand, 1999, p. 127). The SSRIs (Prozac, Paxil, Effexor, Zoloft, etc.) are now the most widely prescribed drugs for panic disorder, with the same side effects—sexual dysfunction, nausea, and insomnia, to name a few. Whichever drugs are given for panic attacks, relapse is very likely once medication is stopped. Unlike behavioral treatments, drug "treatments" do nothing to teach the sufferer coping or breathing skills or relaxation, or that the many situations associated with panic are not the cause of panic.

Behavioral Treatment for Panic Disorder and Agoraphobia

The main components of behavioral treatment for the behavioral problems of panic attacks and agoraphobia include education about the nature of anxiety, panic, and, if applicable, agoraphobia; reappraisal of anxiety-provoking events and situations; repeated exposure to bodily sensations associated with fear or "interoceptive exposure"; exposure with escape prevention (ERP) to external situations associated with panic; and, finally, systematic relaxation and breathing training (e.g., Ballenger, 1999; Barlow & Durand, 1999; Schmidt, Koselka, & Woolaway-Bickel, 2001). In this behavioral "panic control treatment," people with panic problems learn that while attacks may be uncomfortable, they are not life threatening and *are* controllable. In short, the behavioral treatment teaches them effective coping skills.

To expose the panic sufferer to bodily sensations, the sufferer may be asked to run in place to elevate the heart rate and then may be spun in a chair to produce dizziness (e.g., Barlow & Durand, 1999 p. 127). Once this "mini panic" is induced, the sufferer can reappraise the threat (there is none) and practice relaxation and controlled breathing behaviors. The sufferer also will engage in gradual exposure exercises. Studies have found find these approaches highly effective (around 80% of patients see substantial improvement).

However, because stressors, problems, and fears are an inescapable reality of life, like *all people*, anxiety will return to those with panic problems. But for the person who has had behavioral training in dealing with anxiety, stress, and fear, the problems will be less severe and more manageable. Furthermore, unlike the drug approach, which simply teaches people to reach for a pill or bottle to deal with anxiety and fear, the behavioral approach utilizes helpful coping mechanisms that allow the person to confront and overcome fears. If the individual finds that the fear and panic are again becoming overwhelming, then a few "booster sessions" usually enable her or him to reestablish control over fear and anxiety (Brown & Barlow, 1995).

Comparing or Combining Drug and Behavioral Approaches

In a review of "current treatments of the anxiety disorders in adults," psychiatrist James Ballenger reports that for panic disorder "Meta-analyses suggest that CBT [cognitive behavioral therapy] is certainly as effective as, if not more effective than, pharmacotherapy" (1999, p. 1581). This is an understatement! A metaanalysis of 43 studies of panic disorder (people with all levels of agoraphobic avoidance) found that CBT with interoceptive exposure had an effect size of .88; CBT had an effect size of .68; combining drug and behavioral treatments had an effect size of .47; and drugging alone, "pharmacological treatment," had an effect size of .56. Furthermore, CBT had a dropout rate of 5.6%, while combined therapy had a dropout rate of 19.8%, and drugging alone had a dropout rate of 22% (Gould, Otto, & Pollack, 1995). Stated simply: For panic with agoraphobia, behavioral treatment was found to be almost twice as effective as drug treatment and, perhaps because of adverse side effects, four times as many people in the drug "treatment" quit therapy!

Similarly, in the APA's book *Combined Treatments for Mental Disorders*," effect sizes of all of the behavioral treatments are reported to be much higher than the effect size of the most effective drug treatment (SSRIs) (Schmidt et al., 2001, pp. 84, 86). This finding is particularly significant, because the APA is pushing state and national legislators to give psychologists the legal authority to prescribe drugs (a bad idea in my opinion).

Since behavioral treatments are repeatedly found to be far more effective than drug treatments, one may ask why drug treatments are used at all, and is it good to combine them with behavioral approaches? There are several answers.

A cynical answer that nevertheless contains more than a morsel of truth is that the drug companies spend millions and millions of dollars pedaling their products—drugs—and that this advertisement and aggressive promotion work. If it did not work, then advertising would not be a multibillion dollar industry, Britney Spears would have no fans, Bob Dole would not drink Pepsi, and ineffective drug treatments would not be pushed on the unsuspecting public when more effective treatments are available.

But in fairness, and for progress to occur, when a new treatment possibility is offered, such as an SSRI drug, then it should be tested. In addition, when a treatment is shown not to be effective, such as psychoanalysis, or less effective than other available treatments, as drugs are less effective than behavioral approaches, then the most effective treatment available should be adopted and promoted by the treatment community. To do otherwise is unethical.

Finally, in difficult cases where a problem may not be improving with one treatment, or it appears that treatment in a particular case will be especially difficult, it may seem logical to combine treatments. Indeed, this appears to be one of the premises behind the APA's drive for drugs. However, in the case of panic problems ("panic disorder with or without agoraphobia"), combining drugs and behavioral treatment is not best.

Consistency is important; one can be sure that with drugs, treatment is consistent: 10 milligrams of Prozac is 10 milligrams of Prozac is 10 milligrams of Prozac, regardless of who prescribes it or where it is taken. But although effective behavioral treatments exist (and are more effective than drugs), and consistent protocols are becoming available, the "behavioral treatment" received may be highly variable depending on the professional who delivers the treatment. Thus if a person with panic problems goes to an emotionally cold, cynical, belittling therapist who is frankly incompetent at ERP and panic control therapy, then the person is not likely to improve, even though "behavioral treatment" is supposedly occurring. Consistency is one advantage of drugs, but that does not mean drugs should be used, singly or in combination; it does mean that "behavioral therapists" should become more consistent in delivering the empirically proven effective behavioral treatments.

Combining treatment is not the answer to panic problems. According to Ballenger: "In the most recent and best designed controlled multi-center trial, the combination [of behavioral treatment and imipramine, brand name Tofranil] provided little added benefit."

Furthermore, continued Ballenger: "Consistent with other literature at follow-up, more imipramine patients had relapsed 6 months after ending treatment" (1999, p. 1581). More telling is the APA's book on combined treatment. Under *long-term efficacy* for panic disorder, the chapter authors write:

> Studies evaluating long-term efficacy indicate that the pre-liminary benefits of combined treatment are lost during follow-up and that, in some cases, combined treatment may yield poor outcome in the long term...patients receiving combined treatment, despite initial improvements, displayed poorer outcome at follow-up relative to those receiving psychological treatment alone....In summary, data suggest that combined treatments may promote beneficial effects in the short term. In the long term, however, combined treatments may lose their advantage and in some cases (i.e., the combination of exposure plus benzodiazepines) may have deleterious effects. (Schmidt et al., 2001, p. 88)

In their summary of panic disorder treatments, although writing in a book published by an organization (the APA) fighting for prescription privileges, based on the evidence these authors must conclude that "combined treatments cannot currently be recommended" (Schmidt et al., 2001, p. 90). In sum, as is the case generally across the spectrum of behavioral difficulties, and with panic disorder specifically, behavioral approaches are better than drugging people; furthermore, drugging people while they are getting behavioral treatment does not have any benefit. If anything, the opposite occurs—it is harmful.

Chapter 5

OCD
Obsessive-Compulsive Behavioral Problems

People given the label "obsessive-compulsive disorder," or "OCD," have excessive, unwanted, intrusive, repetitive thoughts, and they engage in excessive, repeated, ritualized behaviors. These aversive obsessions and compulsive behaviors can become so excessive that the person who suffers from them is unable to function normally in society (e.g., hold down a job or maintain friendships). If you wash your hands after every trip to the bathroom, before every meal, and after every time you come in from outside, then it is not likely you would be considered obsessive compulsive. But if you cleaned your apartment for 4 hours every day, took 12 showers a day, or washed your hands 50 times a day until they bled, but continued washing, then you would likely be labeled an OCD "cleaner." If you checked to see if your doors were locked and set your alarm and got into bed, only to get out of bed a few minutes later to recheck your doors and alarm, then it is not likely you would be labeled "OCD." But you would likely be labeled an OCD "checker" if you checked every door and every window (downstairs and upstairs, winter and summer) every night, exactly 15 times, and checked every appliance, even ones that had not been used in weeks, in the same order every night, exactly 15 times, and if you got out of order, you started over again.

The drug companies would like us to believe that OCD is "caused" by a "chemical imbalance in the brain," and that it is best treated by the SSRI drug brain whitewash. But having obsessive thoughts and engaging in compulsive behaviors are things people *do*. They are *learned behaviors*. People labeled "OCD" believe that some thoughts and overt behaviors are unacceptable. Often an early experience or teaching is responsible for these beliefs, such as a childhood illness that was believed to be caused by uncleanliness and perceived as life threatening, or a fundamental religious teaching—"masturbation is a mortal sin."

Regardless of the initial source(s) of the unwanted thoughts, the very act of trying to suppress the thought will make it more frequent and intrusive (Salkovskis & Campbell, 1994). To illustrate, do *not* think about Tom Cruise in his underwear. What did you just imagine? For people suffering with obsessive-compulsive behavioral problems, however, the obsessions are perceived as very real and felt as very aversive—germs causing infection and death, one's family burning alive due to a fire from a faulty electrical appliance, burning in hell forever for imagining one's teacher while masturbating. Because the obsessions are aversive, the sufferer tries not to have them. But the more the person tries to suppress the thoughts, the more intrusive they become. Thus behaviors meant to escape the obsessions or avoid the perceived disastrous consequences are performed and rapidly become rituals or compulsions. That is, for the person suffering from obsessions, the compulsions are believed to serve a purpose, to be functional. The compulsions escape or avoid the obsessions' catastrophic consequences—technically speaking, the compulsions are maintained by negative reinforcement. Once the ritual is completed, there may be a temporary feeling of relief or appeasement. Often the compulsions become so entrenched that the original real or imagined reasons for engaging in the ritual may be forgotten. The compulsions seem to "take on a life of their own." Even if the reasons for the compulsions are lost, the sufferer feels extreme anxiety or even guilt until the ritual is performed, which in turn produces a reduction in anxiety.

AN EXPERIMENTAL MODEL

The development of phobias is identical to what happens in "signaled avoidance," and the obsessive-compulsive problem is nearly identical to the "unsignaled avoidance" experimental paradigm that experimental psychologists have been studying for almost 50 years. In signaled avoidance, a light is turned on, followed 10 seconds later by a mild electrical shock to the experimental animal. But if the rat goes into another experimental chamber in less than 10 seconds after the light comes on, the rat avoids the shock. Thus the rat develops a "phobic fear" of the light. Every time the light comes on the rat will do whatever possible to escape the light. To extinguish the rat's fear, the rat is exposed to the light for extended periods, without being shocked and without being allowed to escape. This is exactly the same exposure-and-response prevention treatment that is used in therapy to help people overcome their phobias (see the chapter on phobias).

In unsignaled avoidance, no light or signal comes on before the rat is shocked. The rat is simply shocked randomly at the rate of about 3 shocks every 20 seconds. The rat has no way to know exactly when it will be shocked. However, if the rat presses a lever it can avoid all shocks for a brief period of time, about 30 seconds. Some rats never learn to press the lever, but many do. Those rats that do learn to press the lever, if allowed, will press that lever for the rest of their lives. The rats' lever pressing is "obsessive compulsive."

Persons labeled "OCD" cleaner are obsessed with dirt, germs, and sickness and will compulsively clean even if they have not been dirty or sick for years. Likewise, a rat in unsignaled avoidance will lever press indefinitely, even if it has not been shocked in a long time; the rat is obsessed with the possibility of being shocked and thus compulsively presses the lever. Even if the shock device is turned off, the rat will continue pressing.

But the experimental psychologist can get the rat to stop pressing the lever, and it is not by whitewashing the rat's brain with an SSRI drug. Exposure and response prevention (EX/RP) is used to eliminate the compulsive lever pressing. In EX/RP the shock device is turned off and the rat is placed in the experimental cage, but the lever is either removed or locked so that it cannot be pressed. Thus the rat is exposed to the anxiety, fear, and obsession-producing environment but is prevented from performing its escape and avoidance response. Through basic conditioning, the rat's anxiety, fear, and obsessions, its "need" or urge to press the lever, become extinct—the obsession-compulsive behavior dies out. As the rat is no longer shocked, eventually its fear dissipates, and it no longer "feels the need" to press when the lever is later unlocked. This experimental EX/RP procedure forms the basis for the clinical EX/RP procedures and effectively eliminates obsessive-compulsive behaviors in humans labeled "OCD."

EFFECTIVENESS AND RATIONALE OF
BEHAVIORAL TREATMENT

The behavioral treatment of obsessive-compulsive behavioral treatment is simply the most effective treatment possible. Judy Lam, University of California-San Francisco, and Gail Steketee, Boston University (2001), reviewed and summarized the rationale, method, and effectiveness of behavioral treatment (EX/RP):

> In the first of the two phases, behavioral learning theory asserts that obsessions, like phobias, may be acquired by an association of a neutral cue with an unpleasant or traumatic event, or by observation, or informational learning. Through such an association, innocuous objects such as toilets, appliances, or knives, and thoughts and images such as the devil, gain the power to arouse intense anxiety. Such conditioning need not occur in conscious awareness (e.g., Eelen, 1995)....In the second phase of OCD symptom development, active avoidance or escape strategies (compulsions) that reduce the intense anxiety are likely to be repeated in subsequent situations. Such mental or behavioral rituals are thereby reinforced and become established anxiety management strategies.... [Therefore] the most widely studied behavioral approach used in the treatment of OCD includes exposure in vivo (i.e., in the person) and ritual (response) prevention. In this method, the patient is brought into contact with a feared object (e.g., toilets, door handles, stoves, door locks)...[and] the patient is asked not to engage in his or her usual ritualistic behavior.... Exposure treatments allow patients to face anxiety-provoking material, [and] blocking treatments halt patients' behavioral and/or mental rituals through thought stopping, aversion therapy, distraction, and ritual prevention.... Thus, treatment should habituate obsessive fears and prevent rituals that interfere with anxiety reduction. (p. 159)

How Effective Is This Approach? According to Lam and Steketee:

> Long considered an intractable [noncurable] disorder, OCD has responded well to the combination of direct exposure and

ritual prevention (p. 159)....This combined strategy [EX/RP] has produced gains in approximately 75 percent of OCD patients enrolled in clinical research studies and has led to substantial clinical improvement in most of these individuals. This improvement usually persists at follow-up intervals....[In fact] numerous subsequent studies, both open and controlled trials [of] over 600 patients diagnosed with OCD from several countries, reported that approximately 65 percent to 80 percent of their patients experienced OCD symptom improvement, with 75 percent of these maintaining their gains. (2001, p. 162)

The Behavioral Approach Is Much More Effective Than Drugging People

When pharmacological methods for OCD are compared to behavioral methods, there *is* no comparison. Referring again to Lam's and Steketee's (2001) report:

The best studies of these medications, clomipramine [a tricyclic antidepressant that increases serotonin activity, as do the SSRIs], has yielded average improvement rates in OCD symptoms ranging from 20 to 60 percent after 4 to 12 weeks [compared to 65% to 80% improvement for behavioral treatment!]....Rates for fluoxetine [Prozac] and fluvoxamine [Lovox] are approximately comparable [i.e., results are poor at best]....[Furthermore] apart from problems presented by side effects, results from at least one trial indicate 89 percent of clomipramine responders relapsed even with a duration of 27 months on the drug treatment. (p. 173)

In other words, what Lam and Steketee reported was that even after over 2 years of being drugged, *less than 11% were helped!*

Caution!

Many psychiatrists combine behavioral and drug treatment, operating on the assumption that if behavioral therapy is effective and drugging people might help, even if it is just a little, then the best approach may be to combine the two. However, adding drugs does not increase behavioral treatment effectiveness, even after 6 years (see, e.g., O'Sullivan, Noshirvani, Marks, Monteiro, & Lelliott, 1991). Likewise, "van Balkom et al. (1997) found no advantage to adding fluvoxamine to either EPR [exposure and response prevention] or cognitive therapy, compared to administering these psychological treatments without the medication" (Antony & Swinson, 2001, p. 72). "Nevertheless, many experts advocate combined procedures as the treatment of choice for OCD" (Franklin & Foa, 2002, p. 379). In fact, combining drugs and behavioral treatment for OCD may be harmful. Referring a final time to Lam's and Steketee's (2001) report:

> A recent report by Foa and colleagues (1993) provided preliminary evidence that the addition of clomipramine to exposure treatment *actually impeded progress*, possibly because attribution of gains to medications rendered patients less likely to utilize learning occurring during exposure and ritual prevention practice. (p. 174, italics added)

Drugging people may interfere with their ability to learn. Yet the drug company pushers are likely to counter that the majority of these findings compare clomipramine, an "older" medication, and not the new "miracle" SSRI drugs. But like the pushers' other arguments, this argument is without merit—contradicted by direct comparisons. For example, University of Pennsylvania researchers compared the effectiveness of EX/RP treatment with and without SSRIs (all of the SSRIs, Prozac, Paxil, Zoloft, etc., were represented in the clinical sample). The clinical researchers found that "Both groups made clinically significant and comparable posttreatment gains, suggesting that CBT is effective with or without concomitant pharmacotherapy" (Franklin et al., 2002, p. 162).

The conclusion at this point is clear: If drugging people with obsessive-compulsive behavior problems produces no benefit above behavioral treatment alone, then it is likely unethical to drug such unfortunate people. And, if for some inexplicable reason a person is first put on drugs such as Prozac instead of given behavioral treatment, then the ethical thing to do is add behavioral treatment, because it works. Researchers in the Netherlands found that "supplemental CBT [EX/RP] for OCD patients, after initial, unsuccessful fluoxetine [Prozac] treatment is... effective" (Kampman, Keijsers, Hoogduin, & Verbraak, 2002, p. 314). Why not *start* with what is effective?

Yes, There Is a Brain Difference, but Behavior Changes Brain, Not Vice Versa

In the 1990s, Jeffrey Schwartz and his research team at UCLA excited the psychological and medical communities with their groundbreaking findings. Using positron emission tomography (PET) scans, Schwartz's team found that, yes, part of the brain of OCD patients *was* overactive—a very small area called the "caudate nucleus." Furthermore, this overactivity was likely related to a biochemical imbalance. Of course, this is what the drug companies had been claiming all along. One might expect that the drug companies would be publicizing this finding very aggressively, but they were silent, because what was found to return the caudate to normal levels of activity was *behavior therapy, not drugs*! According to *Newsweek's* account:

> The most popular treatment for OCD is Prozac or a similar drug. Some 30 percent of OCD patients do not respond well to the drug, *and if a patient stops the pills the symptoms return.* But last week, Schwartz and four UCLA colleagues reported in *Archives of General Psychiatry that* ... behavioral modification (changing the way patients act) and cognitive therapy (changing how they think) can *alter the biology of their brains.* PET scans of brain activity after therapy show markedly decreased activity in the "are-you-sure-the-stove-is-off?" caudate. (Begley & Biddle, 1996, p. 60, italics added)

The Schwartz team's conclusion concurred with *Newsweek's* account: "These results replicate and extend previous findings of changes in caudate nucleus function with behavior therapy for obsessive-compulsive disorder" (Schwartz, Stossel, Baxter, Martin, & Phelps, 1996, p. 109). Subsequently Schwartz's team found that the more severe the obsessive compulsion and the more overactive the associated brain areas, the *less* effective drug therapy was compared to behavior therapy! This is of course the exact opposite of what the drug companies would like to be able to claim. "We found that 'higher' pre-treatment metabolic activity in the left OFC [brain circuitry associated with the caudate] was associated with a better response to BT ... medication is less effective in subjects with more severe illness. ... These PET findings are consistent with clinical findings, which indicate that more severe OCD at baseline is predictive of poorer outcome with medication" (Brody, Saxena,

Schwartz, Stoessel, Maidment, Phelps, & Baxter, 1998, p. 4). A white-wash can only do so much, and when it comes to SSRIs and OCD, it is not much indeed.

Behavior Therapy in Private Practice, away from the Ivory tower

While it is absolutely clear that properly conducted behavior therapy is the most effective treatment for obsessive-compulsive behavior problems, it requires much effort and time. Therefore, how it will be applied away from the research institutions is a concern. Conversely, 200 milligrams of Prozac, Zoloft, or Praxil is 200 milligrams, no matter where it is taken or who prescribes it. But behavioral therapists can vary widely.

The question is: will behavior therapy work in private practice? The answer is yes. In "Cognitive-Behavior Therapy of Obsessive-Compulsive Disorder in Private Practice: An Effectiveness Study," Rick Warren and Jay Thomas (2001) examined the effectiveness of behavioral therapy (EX/RP) in a private practice setting and found that "84% of clients showed clinically significant change on obsessions,... and 85% on total Y-BOCS [Yale-Brown Obsession-Compulsion Scale].... There were no differences in degree of change between clients taking medications and those who were not" (p. 281). Thus in routine private practice, behavioral therapy is very effective, and drugs have no bearing on behavior therapy's effectiveness. Wherever people that have problems with obsessions and compulsions are being treated, they should be given behavioral therapy, not drugs.

Chapter 6

ADD and ADHD

Attention deficit disorder (ADD) or attention-deficit hyperactivity disorder (ADHD), is *supposedly* a brain-based disorder (i.e., a "disease") marked by attention deficits and/or hyperactivity. However, there is no conclusive evidence that there is any brain, chemical, or other physiological problems or malfunctioning associated with people labeled "ADD" or "ADHD." Some researchers argue that, *on average*, there may be some slight neurophysical or neurochemical differences between those "with" ADHD and others. "On average," means that many individuals supposedly "have" ADHD but have completely normal neurophysical and neurochemical profiles. Of course, *all* people suffering from a *real* disease have the problematic physical profile. *All* diabetics have *identifiable* insulin deficiencies that reduce or prevent cell glucose absorption and utilization.

The drug companies' greatest success in deceiving Americans has been the almost unquestioned success in convincing doctors, school personnel, and parents that ADHD is a real and chronic problem best treated with drugs (it is not). The fact is, children and adults who have attention and activity problems have *behavior problems*. The best way to improve behavior is with behavior modification techniques, particularly reinforcement-based approaches.

SNAILS AND PUPPY DOG TAILS

The psychological literature on ADHD frequently evaluates whether or not treatment results in "normalization" of ADHD "symptoms" or behaviors. Not surprisingly, drugging children into compliance is often found to produce the greatest "normalization." But what is normal, and who wants to be normal? The largest lobbying group for ADHD, Children and Adults with Attention-Deficit Disorders (CHADD), which has received the vast majority of its funding from Novartis (previously Ciba-Geigy), the company that produces Ritilan (who is in bed with whom?), claims that Benjamin Franklin, Winston Churchill, Socrates, Sir Isaac Newton, Leonardo da Vinci, and many other famous achievers all suffered from ADHD (Wallis, 1994). If CHADD and Novartis had their way, all of these people would have been drugged into normalcy. If they had been drugged, it is unlikely that any of them would have achieved greatness.

All people have their strengths and weaknesses. High activity levels and easily shifting attention are important assets for occupations from hunting to stock trading to ranching. But for sitting still in the classroom and working on monotonous, dull, boring, unrewarding tasks for extended periods of time, high physical activity levels and easily shifting attention often are liabilities rather than strengths. However, that does not make high activity and shifting attention a disorder for which millions of children need to be drugged. With the ever-increasing demands of modern education over the past several hundred years, children's environments have changed—from the unstructured guidance of parents and mentors, to one-room schoolhouses a few hours a day a few months a year, to rigidly structured formal education in confined environments lasting most of the day for most of the year. Even children's "free time" is no longer free—highly scripted activities such as soccer practice, band practice, or a rigid "play date" allow little behavioral flexibility. *Children have not changed*—they have not become hyperactive or developed attention deficits—*but children's environments have changed*, no longer permitting high levels of activity or rapid shifts of attention. Children's behavior is not abnormal; their environment places abnormal demands and restrictions on their behavior. This changed environment has been documented by family practice physician Leonard Sax, MD, PhD:

> Sax has documented a shift in the kindergarten and early elementary curriculum during the past 10 to 20 years, from a play-based curriculum to a more academically oriented curriculum.... This shift to a more academic curriculum in early elementary education may be partly responsible for the

increased propensity of teachers to suggest the diagnosis of ADHD, as well as the increased willingness of parents to consider stimulant medication for their children. An academically oriented kindergarten, in which 5-year-old children are expected to sit at a desk and do paper-and-pencil exercises, poses a major challenge for some children, *when in fact the child may have no underlying psychopathology but merely needs a more developmentally appropriate curriculum.* (Sax & Kautz, 2003, p. 173, italics added)

Of course, in classrooms children's behavior does need to be changed. Learning patience and learning to concentrate are two of education's great lessons. But the classrooms need to be changed too. Classrooms and teachers need to change so the environment and lessons are structured to meet the behavioral skills that children bring to school with them. Children, primarily boys, should not be drugged simply to make teachers' and parents' job easier—but this is *exactly* what is happening. "The amount of methylphenidate (e.g., Ritalin, Concerta) prescribed in the United States increased by more than 500% between 1991 and 1999, while the prescribing of amphetamines (e.g., Dexedrine, Adderall) increased by more than 2000% during the same interval" (Sax & Kautz, 2003, p. 171). Has children's behavior gotten 2000% worse during this time, requiring such medication, or have drug companies' profits soared?

From birth, children have different activity and reactivity levels. For example, the same noise may make one infant twin startle and cry but barely elicit a smile from her twin. A parent's disapproving look may be all the correction one child may ever need, but the child's sibling may seem incorrigible. Yet the equation all too infrequently used—"different + difficult = disorder, therefore drugging is in order"—is a disgraceful disservice. The child's environment and behavioral consequences need to be changed, primarily parenting and educational practices.

Unfortunately, American education is not based on scientifically established principles of learning and skill acquisition (such as reinforcement of successive approximations or reinforced repetitions past perfection; see Flora, 2004). As laid out by Christina Hoff Sommers in *The War against Boys* (2000), U.S. modern education establishment and colleges of education are centered on the romanticism of French philosopher Jean-Jacques Rousseau. This romanticism argues against class structure, reinforcing correct answers, and rewarding appropriate behavior and instead espouses such concepts as "spontaneous virtue," suggesting "student-centered learning." While romanticism sounds noble, it does not work—especially for boys.

Since many of the nation's education colleges espouse feel-good psychobabble rather than equip future teachers with proven systematic reinforcement-based approaches to learning and behavior, it is no surprise that many of today's classrooms are "out of control." Teachers have simply not been taught *how* to control or *how* to teach highly active, rough boys. Thus it is not surprising that teachers eagerly encourage parents to give their children a magic little pill that will make teachers' jobs easier.

This educational practice is unacceptable. Boys are diagnosed as "having" ADHD four times as frequently as girls (e.g., Barlow & Durand, 1999); consequently, most of these boys are drugged. But the reality is, most of these boys simply should have been diagnosed as being "boys." Males and females, boys and girls, *are different*. The scientific evidence is overwhelming that all male primates, including human primates, are significantly more rough-and-tumble, aggressive, and active, and they shift attention more frequently than females. This difference is not simply a product of socialization, as some feminists claim. There *are* subtle neurological differences and not-so-subtle hormonal differences between the sexes that predispose males to higher levels of activity and roughhousing (see Sommers, 2000, for review). America is drugging boys for the "disorder" of being boys. Proper structure, pacing, and reinforcement practices can effectively educate America's youth, female and male—without drugs.

"SYMPTOMS"

To be diagnosed as having ADHD as least six of the so-called symptoms of either inattention or hyperactivity-implusivity must to be present. These "symptoms" (my comments are bracketed) include the following:

Inattention:

a) often fails to give close attention to details or makes careless mistakes in schoolwork, work, or other activities. [This often describes most children.]

b) often has difficulty sustaining attention in tasks or play activities. [This often describes most adults as well as most children.]

c) often does not seem to listen when spoken to directly. [This often "seems" to describe most people.]

d) often does not follow through on instructions and fails to finish schoolwork, chores, or duties in the workplace (not due to oppositional behavior or failure to understand instructions). [Depending on who is doing the evaluating, this often may describe most people.]

e) often has difficulty organizing tasks and activities [This describes many successful people. Organization is a learned skill. If it has not been taught, then that is a failure of teachers and parents, not the child.]

f) often avoids, dislikes, or is reluctant to engage in tasks that require sustained mental effort (such as schoolwork or homework). [This describes most humans and other animals in the world! Indeed, the "law of least effort" holds that it is a natural phenomenon for organisms to avoid effort. Humans must be *trained* to embrace effortful tasks (Eisenberger, 1992).]

g) often loses things necessary for tasks or activities (e.g., toys, school assignments, pencils, books, or tools). [This describes many successful people.]

h) is often easily distracted by extraneous stimuli. [This describes many people, especially males. This is why people work in cubicles or private offices, why men do not like to be disturbed while working in their basement shop or garage, and why everyone craves private space, even if it is only the bathroom stall, a.k.a. "my office."]

i) is often forgetful in daily activities [What? I forgot what I was writing about. ADHD, that's right.]

Hyperactivity:

a) often fidgets with hands or feet or squirms in seat. [One only has to go to church, the mall, an office building, or a restaurant to see that this often describes many people of all ages and levels of personal achievement.]

b) often leaves seat in classroom or in other situations in which remaining seated is expected. [What is "expected"? To do what is expected, one must have a history of reinforcement for doing what is expected. Simply telling a child "I expect you to remain in your seat," and then actually expecting the child to do it, is naive.]

c) often runs about or climbs excessively in situations in which it is inappropriate (in adolescents or adults, may be limited to subjective feelings of restlessness). [Who determines which situations are "inappropriate"? This is a matter of training, not drugs. "Subjective feelings of restlessness" can describe all adolescents or adults at one time or another. Such wanderlust is one of the great forces in human achievement. Now we are supposed to drug for it?]

d) often has difficulty playing or engaging in leisure activities quietly. [This often describes most people, especially males. This is a natural state of childhood and adolescence. As one popular t-shirt reads, "If it's too loud, you're too old." Youthful energy is not a disorder.]

e) is often "on the go" or often acts is if "driven by a motor." [This describes most boys.]

f) often talks excessively. [This describes many successful people.]

Impulsivity:

a) often blurts out answers before questions have been completed. [This is a completely normal behavior that describes many people.]

b) often has difficulty waiting turn. [This describes most children, and almost all boys. Basic reinforcement procedures can teach children to wait their turn. If children are drugged into sedation, they might wait their turn, but they have not *learned* to wait their turn.]

c) often interrupts or intrudes on others (e.g., butts into conversations or games). [This is perhaps a somewhat rude but nevertheless normal behavior that describes many people.]

(American Psychiatric Association, 1994, pp. 83–85).

My bracketed comments should make it clear that the vast majority of these "symptoms" are simply normal behaviors of many people, especially boys. Some may be unpleasant, and a person displaying several of these behaviors may be an unpleasant person indeed. But when did we start drugging people simply because they are unpleasant or difficult?

Furthermore, these "symptoms" are purely *subjective, qualitative, and in the eye of the beholder.* What does "often" mean? One spouse may consider sex five times a week not "often" enough, but the other spouse may consider sex once a week "too often." A teacher who has a child who talks out of turn two times a day may think that is "too often" and unacceptable. This teacher may encourage the child's parents to have the child "tested" and put on drugs. Another teacher may have a student who talks out of turn many more times a day but considers the child a "joy" to have in class. In short, *the dependence on the word "often" to define the "symptoms" of ADHD reduces the disorder to one of personal taste, having nothing to do with any scientific, medical, or objective criteria.*

DRUGS

Since ADHD is presumed to be a "disorder," and a "disorder" is not much, if at all, different from a "disease," it is not surprising that, as with other diseases, the recommended "treatment" for ADHD is drugs. Specifically the pharmaceuticals prescribed are central nervous system stimulants: Ritalin, Dexedrine, Adderall, and Dextrostat. Just like cocaine, crack, ecstasy, and methamphetamine, all of the ADHD drugs work on the monoamine neurotransmitter systems that include the neurotransmitter dopamine, norepinephrine, and epinephrine (noradrenaline and adrenaline). In fact, Adderall, Dextrostat, and Dexedrine *are* *amphetamines*! Ritalin is chemically very similar.

That is scary. But do the drugs work? Yes, but they work the same for everyone, ADHD or not. *Amph*etamines *amplify* the monoamines, and in doing so they stimulate the nervous system. A person whose nervous system is highly activated performs better in all tasks. The effects of such drugs have been extensively studied since the 1930s. In *Running on Ritalin*, Lawrence Diller, MD (1998) nicely summarizes the classic paper on this line of research, "The Enhancement of Human Performance by Caffeine and the Amphetamines" by Victor Laties and Bernard Weiss (1981):

> Weiss and Latie's findings seem to portray a wonder drug. They found the amphetamines (including methamphetamine) vastly superior to caffeine at improving human performance in a variety of mental and physical activities. Amphetamine use led to improved vigilance and accuracy in performing

tasks, especially repetitive and boring ones. It also improved the subjects' attitude about performing such tasks. The drug increased physical endurance for both work and sports.... [Improvements] occurred across the board...while 3 percent may seem small, it translates into cutting 7.2 seconds off a runner's time in a four-minute mile—the difference between fame and oblivion.... Administering amphetamine counteracted...boredom or fatigue in dramatic fashion. (pp. 22–23)

The subjects in these studies were athletes and healthy adults, not ADHD children. The drugs "improved vigilance and accuracy in performing tasks, especially repetitive and boring ones." It is no wonder teachers like to have their students on these types of drugs. Instead of developing nonboring, nonrepetitive teaching materials, which would require work and effort, teachers can, and do, recommend drugging children. Furthermore, "while 3 percent may seem small," a 3% increase in an LSAT, an SAT, a GRE, or a medical school entrance examination score can be the difference between being accepted or rejected. Therefore, it is no wonder that some college students steal their younger siblings "meds" to study for and take such tests, nor is it any wonder that there *is* a black market for these abused and misused drugs, or that the Olympics has outlawed the use of these drugs, including Ritalin.

If these universally performance-enhancing drugs are made available to some, then it is only fair that they be made available to all. Why should some people be given such an advantage because they "often" fidget? But these drugs should be available to next to none. That is the fairest and safest course. These drugs do not teach academics or job skills. They only teach that an effective way to change how one behaves or feels is to take drugs. But this lesson omits the many harmful effects of these drugs. The ADHD drugs, like the other monoamine drugs—crack, cocaine, ecstasy, and methamphetamine—*are* addictive and abusable.

"GO PILLS " AND THE ABUSE OF PERFORMANCE-ENHANCING DRUGS

Because amphetamines increase alertness, attention, and endurance, the world's militaries, especially the U.S. military, are the biggest researchers and users of amphetamines. "The drug was used widely during the

Second World War to keep soldiers awake and alert. American, British, German, and Japanese soldiers were issued amphetamine to combat fatigue and heighten endurance" (CBS News Online, November 17, 2004). The U.S. military continues to issue amphetamines, known as "go pills" by the rank and file, to personnel on a regular basis. In 1970, when the astronauts of Apollo XIII were exhausted on the seventh day of their mission and mission commander Jim Lovell was making computer mistakes on the final course computer program, he and the rest of the crew were ordered to take Dexedrine—amphetamines. The crew arrived back on mother earth safely. A U.S. Special Operations document calls amphetamines "part of a new trend that foresees 'performance enhancements' designed to produce 'iron bodies and iron willed personnel'" (Farrell, 2003). Just as horses are given blinders for races, the U.S. military uses amphetamines as chemical blinders to send men into war.

The military's medication management of manpower comes at a price. Pilots were on go pills in the friendly fire incident of April 2002, when four Canadian troops were killed—bombed by U.S. pilots high on amphetamines provided by the U.S. government. Providing these drugs is "SOP"—standard operating procedure. Despite the fact that GlaxoSmithkline, the makers of Dexedrine, warns that the drug has "high potential for abuse," completely healthy U.S. military personnel are regularly pressured by their superior officers to take highly addictive and abusable drugs (Bonne, 2003). For soldiers high on the government-provided uppers—for soldiers strung out on amphetamines—the military now provides 'no-go pills'—sedatives to calm the soldiers and enable them to sleep (Bonne, 2003).

Ironically, while pressure to take amphetamines is SOP, during Desert Storm "some commanders were so alarmed by many pilots' growing addiction to the pills that they ordered their subordinates not to use them" (Miller, 2003). Even more ironically, while the U.S. military provides amphetamines for pilots, amphetamines are *banned* in commercial aviation! The medical Web site WebMD warns that Dexedrine users should "use caution when driving, operating machinery, or performing other hazardous activities."

Yet employees who work long hours, workers who drive, operate machinery, and perform other hazardous activities, such as truck driving, often use and abuse amphetamines because of their endurance-enhancing properties. Long before the military's use of drugs, as a standard personnel management tool and performance booster, Sigmund Freud advocated using stimulants, cocaine specifically, to enhance performance:

> Freud used cocaine...to help him work late at night; it
> helped him stay alert and concentrate for long hours. He
> liked the drug so much that he wrote a scientific paper on it
> ("On Coca") praising its use. Later, when the negative conse-
> quences of the drug took over his life, he publicly reversed his
> position. (Stein, 1999, pp. 26–27)

Cocaine is just like Ritalin, Adderall, Dexedrine, and the rest. It is a drug
that amplifies the brain's neurochemical amine system. David Mclemore
is now a drug counselor, but he used to be a truck driver and methamphetamine addict. During his days as a truck driver, his boss would "give
everybody lines of meth before starting work." The drug gave him
strength and endurance, but "you don't eat, you don't sleep...you get so
wound up" (Nicholson, 2004). Indeed, as loss of appetite and sleeplessness are two effects of stimulant drugs, is it any wonder why they have
long been associated with stunted growth in children?

Thus we come to the crux of the matter. On the one hand, it is clear
that these drugs can enhance performance. That is why the military
makes use of them, and why they are SOP for flights that can last over
16 hours. On the other hand, they are highly abusable and addictive,
and they create numerous problems. That is why *for everyone except children* labeled "ADD/ADHD" and military troops, they are *illegal*. During
wartime, it can be a matter of life and death for pilots to work extended
hours and to remain alert. But nonmilitary pilots can be given proper
rest, proper nutrition, proper breaks, and proper education, *and so can
our active children*! It is time to stop treating children like worn-out
troops in combat. Instead children, even highly active children, should
be treated like the tender, growing, susceptible, innocent humans they
are. Children should be given proper rest, proper nutrition, proper
breaks, and proper education, not drugs.

"KIDDY COCAINE"

Because Ritalin and the other ADD amphetamine drugs such as
Adderall may enhance performance, including academic performance,
they are being abused by high school and college students at alarming
rates. Students who have not been labeled with ADD or ADHD abuse
these stimulants "in an attempt to enhance their powers of concentration
and improve their academic performance" (Weber, 2004). "Vitamin R,"

"Kiddy coke," "Skippy," and "the smart drug" are common dormitory names for the ADD drugs.

If parents believe that drugs are improving their child's academic performance, they may look the other way, even when it is a situation of abuse. This "smart drug" abuse then leads to other abuse. Just as military personnel are given sedatives, or "no-go" pills to "come down" following an amphetamine high, students often smoke marijuana to "come down" following study sessions involving "Vitamin R" (Weber, 2004).

Marijuana is often cited as a "gateway" drug that leads to harder, more illicit drug use. It may be more likely that Ritalin, Adderall, and the other drugs that supposedly treat ADHD open the door to greater drug abuse. There is no doubt that these drugs are being abused in epidemic proportions on college campuses. For example, 20% of University of Wisconsin-Madison students admit taking ADD drugs without a prescription. The U.S. Department of Health and Human Services found that 1.8 million Americans between ages 18 and 25 admitted taking ADD drugs without a prescription (Nichols, 2004). Like Americans who cheat on their taxes or students who admit to cheating on exams, the actual number of students who take ADD drugs illegally is likely much higher than the number of those who admit to the crime. Thus although the numbers are likely underreported, even if they were overreported by 100% they would still reflect a shocking level of drug abuse by America's youth.

The cute nicknames for these powerful drugs hide their abuse potential. According to the U.S. Drug Enforcement Administration, ADHD drugs have been stolen from pharmacies and schools, have been smuggled from Mexico, and have had multistate distribution rings. Parents have devised scams to obtain multiple prescriptions and then have illegally used the drug themselves or sold or traded them (Kollins, MacDonald, & Rush, 2001). Because as a molecule, Ritalin, D-amphetamine, and cocaine are all structurally and pharmacologically very similar, their abuse potential also should be similar. In a review of 60 scientific studies to assess the abuse potential of Ritalin, 48 (80%) of the studies "indicate that methylphenidate [Ritalin] either functions in a manner similar to D-amphetamine or cocaine, or produces a pattern of subjective effects suggestive of abuse potential" (Kollins et al., 2001, p. 611). Given these facts, it is not much of a stretch to claim that *giving a child an ADHD drug is like giving a child crack*! The only real difference may be that because it is smoked, crack cocaine provides an intense immediate but brief high, whereas the ingested ADHD drugs have a more gradual, long-lasting "dose response curve."

PEDIATRICIAN PRESCRIPTIONS AND DRUG HOLIDAYS

Although trained in the medical care of children, but not trained in psychology or behaviorial analysis, pediatricians "often prescribe attention-deficit drugs to patients [children] without performing the rigorous evaluations that mental health specialists do" (Nichols, 2004, p. A16). Rather than performing "rigorous evaluations," or *any evaluation*, for that matter, pediatricians often, if not usually, rely solely on descriptions of the child's behavior from parents or school personnel. Indeed, one large study found that "Teachers were the most likely [46% of the time] to be the first to suggest the diagnosis of ADHD, followed by parents [30%]" (Sax & Kautz, 2003, p. 172). To be clear here, Sax is and Kautz's findings suggest that almost 80% of the children "diagnosed" with ADHD are so "diagnosed" by individuals with *no* training, thus with no ethical business of suggesting a "disorder." It is one thing to say that a child is having problems at school, but it is another to diagnose a child in an effort to have the child be drugged for a disorder. Indeed, previous studies have found that "teachers may have confused ADHD behaviors with other problems, e.g., low IQ, anxiety, [and] psychological stressors" (Nolan, Gadow, & Sprafkin, 2001, cited in Sax & Kautz, 2003, p. 173). Teachers and parents are not trained in psychiatric difficulties but make diagnoses of ADHD in children with other problems, problems that need to be addressed without the use of drugs. In fact, sometimes a prescription can be obtained by a student without even having to see a doctor (see, e.g., Nichols, 2004, p. A42). A pediatrician who gives a child a prescription for an ADHD drug without a rigorous, or any, evaluation is analogous to an orthopedic surgeon prescribing heart disease medication to a man solely based on his wife's description of his difficulties.

Yet while these doctors will prescribe these highly abusable drugs in an almost whimsical fashion, at some level they must recognize that these drugs are highly dangerous and that they "treat" no real disease or disorder. Both the drug companies that make the abusable drugs and the doctors who prescribe them recommend that children on the drugs be given "drug holidays"—times, usually on weekends, holidays, and summer vacations—when the drugs are not taken. Imagine if someone with diabetes, HIV, or severe epilepsy were given a "drug holiday" during these times. The death rate from these disorders would skyrocket.

These "drug holidays" are proof that these drugs do not treat any disorder but simply medicate behavior. Drug children to make them manageable. If these drugs treated a real disorder, then during the drug holidays complications from the disorder would escalate. Instead, during drug holidays, the adverse side effects of the drugs—loss of appetite, insomnia, restlessness, and irritability—subside. If these drugs were really necessary, then holidays would not be necessary or advised.

ATTENTION DEFICITS, DRUGS, AND CRIME

One of the real problems of children who are often inattentive and highly active is that they may frequently break the rules of the home, school, or law. Depending on whether these rule violations are dealt with using consistent, firm behavioral techniques, such as time out from positive reinforcement, response cost (fines), or privilege loss, or are dealt with using destructive, coercive practices and physical punishment will strongly influence whether or not these active, rule-breaking children develop into law-abiding citizens or criminals (see Flora, 2004, pp. 155–180). Children who develop chronic rule-breaking and coercive interpersonal behaviorial patterns often are labeled or "diagnosed" with "oppositional-defiant disorder" or "conduct disorder," and they end up in trouble with the law.

Ironically, instead of psychiatrists teaching these children appropriate conduct by providing suitable reinforcement for good behavior and consistent consequences for misconduct, basing their decision on a large and an influential but a highly flawed study (the MTA, described later), many proclaim that active, inattentive children "with comorbid conduct or oppositional-defiant disorder *require* medication" (Arnold, Chuang, Davies, Abikoff, et al., 2004, p. 50, italics added). As it is true that truck drivers high on amphetamines may drive longer and troops high on amphetamines may follow orders to blindly jump into harm's way, children given these drugs may behave in accordance with the rules, but *only while they are on these drugs*! However, nothing, absolutely nothing, has been done to help these children in the long run.

Drugging children so they follow the rules and pay attention does nothing to teach them how to behave as law-abiding citizens. Behavior modification techniques do teach children how to get along in society. Pioneering work by psychiatrist James Satterfield and psychologist Anne Schell compared rates of criminality over several years in children through young adulthood who were labeled ADD or ADHD and who had been given drug treatment, or a multimodal treatment of both drugs and psychological treatment with an emphasis on behavior modification

(Satterfield, Satterfield, & Schell, 1987; Saterfield & Schell, 1997). With the multimodal treatment, children were taught that "behavior and learning improvements had to be credited to their own active participation in mastering skills, rather than to passive experiencing of medication effects... [and] improved self-esteem was attempted through mastery of skills" (Satterfield, et al., 1987, p. 59). Additionally, "parents were trained to apply behavior modification techniques consistently within the framework of understanding their child's specific behaviors and their consequences. Many parents had to learn appropriate discipline techniques and how to discontinue futile yelling, spanking, or other more abusive forms of punishment" (Satterfield, et al., 1987, p. 59).

The effects of drug treatment compared to the mutlimodal behavioral training were stunning. The mean number of felony arrests for the drug group was twice that of the multimodal group. Further results reveled that "DTO [drug treatment only] subjects were twice as likely as MMT (multimodal treatment] subjects (28% vs. 14%, $p < 0.05$) to have been multiple felony offenders (arrested at least twice) and that the institutionalization rate for the DTO subjects was nearly three times that for the MMT subjects (22% vs. 8%)" (Satterfield et al., 1987, p. 61). The length of time the children were medicated had no effect on arrest records, but the longer the behaviorally oriented treatment was received, the less likely the children were to be arrested. The researchers predicted that the drug-treated children would not have fared better than children given no treatment at all, "given the fact that studies of long-term effectiveness of drugs alone have been consistently discouraging" (p. 62). "Furthermore, it may be that drug treatment alone is ineffective in improving long-term outcome because it does little to improve self-concept, social adjustment, existing educational deficits, or many forms of childhood antisocial behavior" (p. 67). Behavior modification is the proven method of improving long-term outcome, precisely because it specifically addresses social adjustment, existing educational deficits, and many forms of child antisocial behavior (Flora, 2004, pp. 117–197).

WHAT WORKS?

While the long-term effectiveness of drugs for problems of antisocial behavior has been "consistently discouraging," the short- and long-term effectiveness of behavioral techniques has been consistently encouraging. Behavioral approaches to problems of attention and inappropriate activity (e.g., ADD and ADHD) also have consistently been as effective or more effective than any drug "treatment." For example, an early study offering "a behavioral-educational alternative to drug control of hyperactive children" (Ayllon, Layman, & Kandel, 1975) found that during math and reading performance when medication was withdrawn hyperactivity did increase from 20% to 80%. There also was a *slight increase* in math and reading performance when the children were taken *off the drugs*. Yet among the children who were off drugs and given token reinforcement for correct academic responses, hyperactivity decreased to 20% (the same as the drugged level), and correct responding soared from 12% to over 85% correct. Thus drugs may manage hyperactive behavior, but only reinforcement can *motivate* appropriate academic behaviors.

A review of 16 studies examined the "relative efficacy of pharmacological, behavioral, and combination treatments for enhancing academic performance" in "hyperactive, learning disabled, and hyperactive-learning disabled children...concluded that certain academically oriented behavioral interventions were clearly superior to medication and that there was only limited support for the notion stimulant drugs markedly enhance the efficacy of the former" (Gadow, 1985, p. 513). Behavioral interventions that have been proven effective include token reinforcement, where tokens are earned for appropriate behavior, and correct academic performance (the tokens are later exchanged for preferred activities, treats, or toys); response cost—privileges or tokens are lost contingent upon inappropriate behavior; and parent and teacher training in continency management where adults are taught to deliver appropriate reinforcers or punishment (response cost, time-out) in accordance with the child's behavior. Procedures such as these teach children that their behaviors have consequences (good or bad, depending on the appropriateness of the behavior). Consequently, the child's behavior becomes better controlled and more appropriate, and academic performance improves. Drugging a child teaches none of this.

BIG LEAGUES, LITTLE LEAGUES: STIMULANTS AND SPORTS

In 2005, the owners of the major league baseball teams and the players union came to a new agreement concerning testing for steroids and punishments for positive results. However, many reports claim that stimulant abuse is a far worse problem than steroid abuse in baseball, with up to 80% of players taking stimulant drugs before games. Finally, in November 2005, major league baseball "stepped up to the plate" and announced that several stimulants, including amphetamines, would be against the rules in the new agreement. Like high school students taking their younger siblings' ADHD drugs for high-stakes SATs it is easy to understand how major leaguers, who are paid millions of dollars to play a child's game, would be eager to get whatever edge they could in concentration and attentiveness—even if illegal. Attempting to hit hard balls flying toward one's face at almost 100 miles per hour with a piece of wood requires acute attention. Being ready to catch a ball in the outfield at all times, even though it may be hours between balls, requires extended concentration. But athletes are supposed to *train* to gain this necessary acute attention and extended concentration, they are not supposed to take drugs. That is why amphetamines, Ritalin, and other stimulants are illegal in college and Olympic sports, but major league baseball has chosen to apply softer penalties for amphetamine use than for steroid use.

It is unknown how many little league players, parents, and coaches will attempt to imitate the big league's pattern of abusing stimulants to improve performance, or how many will consider drug abuse an acceptable risk to take for getting an (illegal) edge in the keen competition for an athletic scholarship or a minor league contract. However, two small but intensive studies show that when token reinforcements are used as an aid, stimulant use, much less abuse, is unnecessary during sports, unnecessary even for "ADHD-diagnosed children" (Hupp, Reitman, Northup, O'Callaghan, & LeBlanc, 2002; Reitman, Hupp, O'Callaghan, Gulley, & Northup, 2001). In the first study, ADHD-diagnosed "children had the opportunity to earn tokens for paying attention to the game," and a "token was awarded if the participant was in the ready position" prior to a pitch. Tokens were later exchanged for various "goodies" (Reitman et al., 2001, p. 313). On some days the children were on their stimulant medication (Ritalin, Adderall), while on other days they were given placebo pills instead. The children themselves and observers recording the children's behavior did not know if the children had been given a placebo or a drug. The results revealed that "in all cases, the token economy appeared to increase attentive behavior to a greater extent than medication" (Reitman et al., 2001, p. 314). That is, *teaching* and *reinforcing* children to be ready for a pitch are more effective than attempting to drug them to do so. An additional benefit of the reinforcement procedure was that "although the behavioral intervention did not directly target reductions in disruptive behavior, rewarding attentive behavior appeared to have the positive side effect of decreasing disruptiveness" (Reitman et al., 2001, pp. 318–319). The researchers concluded by noting:

> Inasmuch as previous research suggests that athletic competence correlates significantly with social status, interventions directly targeting athletic competence (i.e., sport skills, sportsmanship, game knowledge, and attentive game behaviors) may yet prove an effective complement to social skills training and an important adjunct to existing treatment protocols designed for ADHD-diagnosed children and adolescents. (2001, p. 320)

Only a handful in millions of baseball-playing-children will ever play professionally or in college (even little league "all stars"), but all children will have to *learn* to get along with other people, and parents want their children to be well liked by others, to be "good sports." Reinforcement-based behaviorial procedures can *teach* sportsmanship, but drugs cannot. In the second study, researchers directly reinforced ADHD-diagnosed children's sportsmanshiplike behaviors (e.g., high fives, cheering a teammate, etc.) with tokens; again, on some days the children were given stimulant medication, on other days placebos. Results showed that immediate token reinforcement increased prosocial behavior, but "neither form of stimulant medication (i.e., Ritalin or Adderall) appeared to have a positive effect on prosocial sportsmanlike behavior. . . . The present results support the suggestion that the positive effects of stimulant medication in social settings may be limited to decreasing maladaptive behavior, and more active behavioral programing may be necessary to increase prosocial behavior" (Hupp et al., 2002, p. 159). Children, especially highly active children, cannot be drugged into being good sports or getting along with others. The more active the child, the more directly the child needs to be *taught* good sportsmanship and social skills in general.

THE MTA—"SCIENCE" GONE BAD

Despite the fact that drugging active children has no effect on attentive and disruptive behavior during sports (see, e.g., Reitman et al., 2001), does nothing to teach sportsmanship (Hupp et al., 2002), has no effect on later criminality (see, e.g., Satterfield, Hoppe, & Schell, 1982), and is inferior to behavioral interventions for academic performance (e.g., Gadow, 1985), many, if not most, professionals will argue that not only is drug treatment "proven" to be the most effective treatment for ADHD, it is the *only* treatment needed.

These professionals point to the "Multimodal Treatment Study for Children with Attention-Deficit Hyperactivity Disorder" (MTA) as scientific "proof" that ADHD medication is the best treatment available for ADHD. The standard portrayal of the MTA is that it was a 5-year clinical trial by the National Institute of Mental Health at six academic sites using the latest and best clinical and scientific practices to compare four treatments for ADHD: medication management (MM), behavioral treatment (BT), combined MM and BT, and a community comparison control (CC) group (see, e.g., MTA Cooperative Group, 1999). The highly publicized, but equally highly flawed, results of the study that was designed to find medication superior were just that—medication was found to be superior, and the researchers concluded that although "all 4 groups showed sizable reductions in symptoms over time"

> for ADHD symptoms, our carefully crafted medication management was superior to behavioral treatment and to routine community care that included medication. Our combined treatment [MM and BT] did not yield significantly greater benefits than medication management for core ADHD symptoms, but may have provided modest advantages for non-ADHD symptom and positive functioning outcomes. (MTA Cooperative Group, 1999, p. 1073)

Almost immediately the drug companies began publicizing *these* results of the MTA and sponsoring slick, continuing education symposiums at the annual conventions of the APA and elsewhere. Attendees (I was one) were fed gourmet breakfasts and a steady diet of presentations and pamphlets, all claiming the glorious benefits and superiority of drugging children. Still relatively new, Powerpoint presentations dazzled the crowd with such messages as: "**Myth**—Counseling or Therapy Should Be Tried before Medication; **Fact**—MTA study found medication to be more effective than behavior therapy" (Faraone, 2003).

It is true that the MTA claimed to find medication more effective than behavior therapy, but in the study, behavior therapy was *stopped* for months, while medication was continued. The drug pushers failed to point out this major flaw, this *fatal flaw*, of the study.

The MTA is similar to a study that would claim to compare drugs to a behavioral therapy of modification of exercise and diet in the treatment of high blood pressure. However, after being taught to exercise and diet, participants would be taken off this regime for several months, but those on medication would not be not taken off it before final measures of heart health were made. No one would be surprised to find that the drugs worked better in the "comparison," because in reality there was *no* comparison between drugs and behavior therapy, and in reality there was *no* comparison between drugs and behavior therapy in the MTA. Therefore it is simply untrue to claim that medication was superior to behavior therapy.

Fortunately not all of the researchers in the MTA group bought the overall simplistic flawed—false—finding that MM was superior to BT. Principally among them, William Pelham, PhD, exposed "facets of the design that *predisposed the study* in favor of a differentially positive outcome for pharmacological relative to behavioral treatment" (Pelham, 1999, p. 981, italics added). Not only did the design predispose a favorable outcome for medication, and in so doing invalidate those very findings, when the methods and results are examined critically it is again found that behavioral treatment is the treatment of choice for highly active children labeled with ADHD.

In the MTA the children in the MM and combined MM and BT group were medicated with methylphenidate hydrochloride (the active amphetamine of several ADHD drug brands). A damning finding regarding these groups was that "although both groups started at the same point, the combined group did not have doses increased over the 14 months of treatment, while the MM group had doses increased by 20%—all due to deterioration of functioning at monthly checks" (Pelham, 1999, p. 984). That is, those children who were only put on drugs had *deteriorative functioning*. To compensate for this, drugs were increased. Conversely, the children who were drugged but also had behavior therapy did not have to have their dosages increased; their functioning did not deteriorate, because the behavior therapy worked. It is a disgrace that drugging is psychiatry's recommended first line of treatment for highly active children.

BEHAVIOR THERAPY IN THE MTA

The behavior therapy in the MTA was initiated in a summer treatment program (STP) at Pittsburgh, California-Irvine, and California-Berkeley universities and was provided to children in the BT and combined treat-ment groups of the MTA. The STP included a point system whereby children earned points for appropriate behaviors and lost points for inap-propriate behaviors. Points were exchanged for privileges and honors. In addition to sporting activities, children spent 1 hour in special educa-tion, 1 hour in a computer-assisted instruction classroom and 1 hour a day in art. Parents received weekly behavioral parent training that demonstrated the proper use of reinforcement systems and time-out, as well as how to implement home rewards based on their child's daily report card (DRC). Children received DRCs that targeted individualized behaviors for each child, and parents were to reward their child with privileges if the child met the goals on the DRC (Pelham, Gorgy, Greiner, Hoza, Hinshow, Swanson, Simpson, Shapiro, Bukstein, Baron-Myak, & McBurnett, 2000).

Following the STP, the children's regular teachers were encouraged to continue DRCs, but parent training was reduced from once a week to monthly (a fourfold decrease), teacher consultation was reduced as drasti-cally and more haphazardly, and contingency (reinforcement) manage-ment went from the STP and counselors to a paraprofessional teacher's aide during the fall *to nothing* during the winter and spring (Arnold et al., 2004, p. 40). Following this drastic reduction and then elimination of the behavior therapy, while in the medication groups medication was still being maintained (indeed, while medication was being *increased*), com-parisons were made between behavior therapy and drugging children.

Specifically, the effects of the pharmacological treatments were assessed at posttreatment while subjects were actively med-icated; in contrast, the effects of BT were assessed following fading of therapist involvement. The intensive period of the BT ended in late December or early January, and endpoint measures were typically taken 4 to 6 months later—usually several months after the last planned, face-to-face, therapeutic contact. Thus, the endpoint MTA treatment comparison was for *active* MM treatment versus *withdrawn* BT....It could be argued that such outcomes [e.g., the supposed superiority of medication] were *predetermined*, given the study design.... *Had the study been designed so that medication had been faded while intensive BTs had continued, the results may very likely have been reversed.* (Pelham, 1999, pp. 981–83, italics added)

Temporary Drug Effects versus Lasting Behavior Therapy

Drug effects last only a few hours at most and then have *no* benefit. Because while the child is being drugged it is less likely that active, effective, lasting behavioral therapy will be applied, the effects of drugging a child for high activity may actually be harmful. Pelham and his coauthors have documented other related problems with the use of stimulants:

> First, stimulants have not been shown to produce long-term changes in achievement or long-term prognosis.... Furthermore, the beneficial effects of stimulants stop as soon as the medication wears off, 3–10 [hours] depending on the preparation.... [And] despite the fact that stimulants would need to be used for years with most ADHD individuals, most parents give their children medication for only a few months. (Pelham et al., 2000, p. 508)

It is relatively easy to give a child a pill with breakfast, and perhaps one at lunch. And frankly, although it is very effective, active daily behavior management can be a pain for teachers and parents, resulting in "failure" of behavior modification:

> In many cases, such failure may be attributable to treatment noncompliance on the part of parents and teachers. Because it is more time-consuming, difficult, and expensive for parents, regular classroom teachers, and agencies to conduct behavioral systems relative to medication, adults and agencies may not expend the effort necessary to conduct good behavioral interventions. (Pelham et al., 2000, p. 508)

Although it may be easier to medicate, that does not make it right. Furthermore, as appropriate behavior increases and inappropriate behavior decreases under behavior management, behavior management becomes easier to implement and becomes more reinforcing for the parents and teachers as their efforts bring success. Indeed, although still arguing for active medication, several of the MTA researchers found that behavior gains were maintained and generalized, *despite the fact that behavioral therapy had been withdrawn,* yielding "continuing improvement" (Arnold et al., 2004).

While behavior therapy can produce continuing improvement, even when withdrawn, *drugs produce immediate deterioration when withdrawn.*

FAIR, HONEST COMPARISONS

An honest comparison between drugging children and providing behavior modification would be to compare them when both are withdrawn and when both are active. Some of these comparisons already have been reviewed. When both were withdrawn, children who had received medication only had over twice the risk of criminal arrest and imprisonment compared to youth who had received behavioral intervention (see, e.g., Satterfield et al., 1982). When both are active, "highly effective academically oriented behavioral interventions are clearly superior to medication" (Gadow, 1985, p. 513). In fact, behavior intervention is very effective in remedying numerous academic and conduct problems related and unrelated to attention and high activity (see Flora, 2004, p. 117–197 for a review). The ADHD medications do not affect such problems.

When the MTA is viewed without an eye predisposed to finding medication superior, viewed by those who do not have their work financially supported by drug companies, and when both are active

> the major finding is that adjunctive stimulant medication produced relatively few incremental gains on acute functioning and had no effect on rate of improvement for children receiving [the behavior therapy of] the STP and parent training.... *The results therefore demonstrate that the MTA results at 14-month outcome (MTA Cooperative Group 1999) showing large incremental effects of medication beyond a faded clinical behavioral intervention were not apparent when the behavioral condition in the study was active and intensive.* (Pelham et al., 2000, p. 520, italics in original)

Because both the BT group and the combined BT and MM group showed the same rates of improvement over the STP while medication remained constant

> improvement in both groups can be [indeed, *must be,*] attributed to the behavioral intervention...medication does not

facilitate the rate at which children improve in a concurrent intensive behavioral treatment.... [Furthermore] when individual target behaviors are considered, unmedicated children experience that same degree of success as do medicated children. (Pelham et al., 2000, p. 520)

Given these findings,

the most parsimonious conclusion, given the present and previous results, is that if a behavioral intervention is sufficiently intensive, then improvement over time and to a less extent absolute levels of functioning are unaffected by concurrent and steady stimulant medication. (Pelham et al., 2000, p. 521)

With this conclusion the researchers addressed the overriding question behind America's drug deception:

The ultimate question of which treatment modality [drugs or behavioral modification] is superior can only be addressed by considering relative costs *and* relative long-term benefits of the interventions. Behavioral treatments are more expensive than medication, but medication alone has no impact on the negative long-term outcome of children with ADHD.... Given the enormous sums currently spent on mental health services for children, most of which are nonefficacious treatments (Weisz & Hawley, 1998), refocusing such expenditures on evidence-based intensive summer camps [or other behavioral treatments] is not unreasonable. (Pelham et al., 2000, p. 523, italics added)

"Not unreasonable" is a large understatement. On the basis of the studies reviewed here it would not be unreasonable to conclude that the *MTA is a poorly designed, drug-company-funded scam to push the use of their highly profitable drugs.* It also is not unreasonable to assume that when parents are properly informed of the *long-term* outcome of drugging their children—none—and the beneficial immediate and long-term outcomes of applying reinforcement-based behavioral modification, most parents would be willing to put forth the extra effort to help their children succeed in life.

Chapter 7

Depression

What Is Depression?

A "major depressive episode" is the most severe and most common type of depression diagnosed by psychiatrists. Their diagnostic "criteria" include a severely depressed mood for "at least" 2 weeks. "Symptoms" include anhedonia (the inability to experience pleasure), appetite or weight change (losses *or* gains), insomnia *or* hypersomnia, and behavioral agitation *or* retardation (e.g., behavioral suppression), and these symptoms result in distress or impaired functioning.

The *American Heritage Dictionary of the English Language,* 3rd edition, defines depression as:

> the act of depressing.... The condition of *feeling* sad or despondent. A psychotic or neurotic condition characterized by an *in*ability to concentrate, *in*somnia, and *feelings* of extreme sadness, dejection, and hopelessness.... A *reduction in activity* or force. A *reduction in physiological vigor or activity....* A *lowering* in amount, degree, or position.... A period of *drastic decline.* (1992, p. 503, italics added)

This dictionary definition comes close to capturing the behavioral view of depression. When something is depressed, it is reduced or suppressed, and there is a reduction or decline from typical levels. When it is said that a person "is depressed," it is not meant that that person has become shorter or weighs less than normal. No, what is meant by "depressed" is that behavior is depressed! A person's activity and resulting feelings are depressed, deactivated, reduced, and suppressed from typical levels. This drastic decline in behavior includes both overt, observable behavior and covert behavior (thoughts and feelings). "Being depressed" often includes both decreases in appropriate, productive, and pleasurable behaviors, such as attending work, family activities, or parties or other outings, and increases in inappropriate and unpleasurable behaviors, such as crying and alcohol abuse.

CAUSES OF DEPRESSION

Productive and pleasurable behavior—like all behavior—becomes depressed when it is punished or not reinforced, and nonproductive, unpleasurable behavior increases when more reinforcement is received *relative* to the reinforcement received for productive, pleasurable activities. When these contingencies are persistent and generalized, an individual may "become depressed."

More specifically, depression often results from "learned helplessness" (see, e.g., Seligman, 1975) or from the *reinforcement of depression* (see, e.g., Lewinsohn, 1974; see Flora, 2004, for a summary and an analysis). In learned helplessness an individual literally learns to be helpless, hopeless, and learns that his or her behavior usually cannot produce pleasurable consequences or avoid aversive consequences. In Seligman's original research on learned helplessness, dogs who had first received uncontrollable shocks in a harness never learned to avoid shocks in a cage when they could have just moved to the other side of the cage. Due to the initial uncontrollable shocks in the harness, the dogs learned to be helpless. Their behavior became depressed. Research with humans has found that previous experience with uncontrollable aversive events often results in learned helplessness, a sense of hopelessness, and depression (see, e.g., Barlow & Durand, 1999, p. 205). Many studies find that stressful life events are highly linked to the development of depression (see, e.g., Kessler, 1997). Sick or injured children who must limit their activities and thus experience decreased rates of reinforcement are at great risk for depression (Lewinsohn, Gottlib, & Seeley, 1997).

If as an infant a person's cries were ignored and as a child drawings and play seldom produced praise and affection, schoolwork was ignored, and attempts at interpersonal socialization were not reinforced, then that person is likely to become depressed—his or her behavior will be depressed. Uncontrollable, aversive, nonreinforcing life events such as childhood experiences of marital conflict, divorce, or death may result in pervasive feelings of hopelessness and are linked to emotional problems, including depression (see, e.g., Kelly, 1998). As behavior becomes depressed, fewer normal, achievement-oriented, proactive, prosocial, *non*depressed behaviors occur, and a self-perpetuating downward spiral into despair is likely (Flora, 2004, pp. 201–202).

Essentially, once a person decreases the rate of productive behaviors, the rate of reinforcement for productive behaviors will consequently decrease, occasioning an even lower rate of productive behaviors—a lowered rate of happiness-producing behaviors. Additionally, behaviors associated with depression—social withdrawal, crying, complaints, statements of despair—may be directly reinforced by the social environment of the depressed person. Lisa Sheeber and her coworkers, in their study of over 400 families with depressed and nondepressed adolescents, theorized the following.

> Depressive behavior may be functional in its capacity to elicit desirable social consequences.... Women's depressive behavior is negatively reinforced by reduced aggressiveness on the part of their spouses and children.... Additionally... depressive behaviors have been found to elicit help and support. (Sheeber, Hops, Andrews, Alpert, & Davis, 1998, p. 418)

This is exactly what they found:

> Mothers were more likely to emit problem-solving and facilitative behaviors in response to adolescent depressive behavior in families of the depressed adolescents than in families of the non-depressed adolescents.... Adolescent depressive behavior was also more likely to suppress paternal aggressive behavior in families of depressed adolescents. This... suggests that depressive behavior may provide a brief respite by decreasing family members' aggressive behaviors. (Sheeber et al., 1998, p. 423)

In sum, the behavioral analysis of depression is that depression results from various combinations of the following:

- experience of uncontrollable aversive life events, producing learned helplessness and hopelessness;

- a low rate of reinforcement for productive, happiness-producing behaviors that feeds back to further deactivate behavior and decrease the rate of productive, happiness behaviors and reinforcers into a spiral of despair; and
- functional effects of depressive behaviors, in that such behaviors elicit help and support (positive reinforcement) and/or suppress hostile and aggressive behaviors of others (negative reinforcement). Depression *is* depressed *behavior* and results from interactions between behavior (primarily social behavior) and the environment.

DRUG ANALYSIS OF DEPRESSION

As with other psychological difficulties, the pushers for drugs as treatment for depression view depression as being caused by a chemical imbalance in the brain. Generally, depression is said to be caused by low levels of monoamine neurotransmitters: serotonin, dopamine, epinephrine, and norepinephrine. Older antidepressant drugs—monoamine oxidase inhibitors and tricyclic anitdepressants—were meant to increase monoamine levels in often unsuccessful attempts to treat depression. The SSRIs—Zoloft, Paxil, Prozac, and the rest—raise serotonin levels.

Studies have found that drugs given for depression *do* alter brain function. But, surprise, surprise, sugar pills or placebos change brain function as well. In "Placebo Alters Brain Function of People with Depression," researchers found that not only did brain function change but 38% of the placebo group improved compared to 52% of the drug group. Thus the powerful nervous system drugs only offered a small 14% improvement over sugar pills. According to lead researcher Andrew F. Leuchter, MD, director of the UCLA Neuropsychiatric Institute and Hospital, "People have known for years that if you give placebos to patients with depression or other illnesses, many of them will get better.... What this study shows, for the first time, is that people who get better on placebo have a change in brain function, just as surely as people who get better on medication" (quoted in Smith, 2002). Imagine how much more these individuals would have been helped had either group been given highly effective behavioral treatment!

If both drugs and placebos change brain function, then one would expect that behavioral treatment would change brain function as well, and it does. When 15 to 20 sessions of CBT were compared to treating depressed individuals with the drug Paxil for 6 weeks, people in both groups reported decreased depression. But "only those participating in CBT showed decreased over-activity in the medial frontal cortex, an area of the brain implicated in self-monitoring and self-assessment. By comparison, the people who took paroxetine [Paxil] showed no change in this area, but they did experience decreased activity in . . . a limbic system region associated with mood regulation" (Dingfelder, 2004). The different brain changes caused by CBT or drugs reflect the way CBT treats depression, while drugging individuals simply whitewashes emotions. Behavioral activation, including self-monitoring, and self-assessment lead to *self-empowerment*, allowing people to lead productive, happy lives. Drugging people to change their moods teaches them that to feel good they need to take drugs. It does not teach them how to be productive or happy. Drugging people depends on the power of chemistry to change moods, making people dysfunctional and depressed. By teaching productive, active life skills, behavioral therapies result in self-empowerment, allowing formerly depressed people to lead productive, uplifting lives, which naturally will lead to happy, nondepressed moods. The evidence is clear that drugs, placebos, and behavioral treatment all produce changes in brain function. This leads us to an important question, the topic of our next section.

DRUGS OR COGNITIVE BEHAVIORAL THERAPY—WHICH IS A MORE EFFECTIVE TREATMENT FOR DEPRESSION?

David Antonuccio of the University of Nevada School of Medicine and Reno Veterans Affairs Medical Center has summarized the meta-analyses comparing CBT to drug treatment:

> The preponderance of the available scientific evidence shows that psychological interventions, particularly coginitve-behavioral therapy (CBTs), are generally as effective or more effective than medications in the treatment of depression, even if severe, for both vegetative and social adjustment symptoms, especially when patient-rated measures and long-term follow-up are considered. . . . A Yale psychiatrist (Wexler & Cicchetti, 1992) who reviewed seven well-controlled outcome studies of

513 individuals concluded that combined treatment offers no advantage over treatment with psychotherapy [e.g, CBT] alone and only modest advantage over treatment with pharmacotherapy alone. When dropout rate is considered with treatment success rates, pharmacotherapy alone is substantially worse than psychotherapy alone or the combined treatment. This meta-analysis suggests that psychotherapy alone should usually be the initial treatment for depression rather than exposing patients to unnecessary costs and side effects of combined treatment. (1995, p. 450)

The other meta-analyses comparing CBT to drug treatment for depression have similar findings, and all point to the same conclusion:

Steinbrueck, Maxwell, and Howard (1983) reviewed 56 controlled depression outcome studies and found a psychotherapy mean effect size of 1.22, whereas the drug therapy mean effect size (treatment mean minus control mean, divided by the control standard deviation) was 0.61 [e.g., psychotherapy was found to be twice as effective as drugs]....Dobson (1989) reviewed 8 controlled outcome studies (N = 721) comparing CBT with tricyclic medications and found that the average CBT patient did better than 70% of drug patients and that the average CBT differential effect size was 0.53 larger than that for drugs. Hollon, Shelton, and Loosen (1991) reviewed 9 randomized controlled outcome studies (N = 542) and found...CBT reduces the risk of relapse compared with drugs. Conte, Plutchik, Wild, and Karasu (1986) reviewed 17 controlled outcome studies (N = 1,009) using combined treatments and found that...100% of the CBT evidence indicated no advantage of combined treatment over psychotherapy alone....Meta-analysis by Greenberg, Bornstein, Greenberg, and Fisher (1992), covering 22 controlled studies (N = 2,230),...calls into serious question the perceived efficacy of tricyclic antidepressant medications, which are shown only to be more effective than inert placebo and only on clinician-rated measures, not patient-rated measures. If patients cannot tell that they are better off in a controlled study, one must question the conventional wisdom about the efficacy of antidepressant drugs. The newer selective serotonin reuptake inhibitors (SSRIs) do not appear to fare much better. (Antonuccio, 1995, pp. 450–51)

Indeed, SSRIs may fare worse. A more recent study conducted by researchers at Duke Univesrity Medical Center (Davidson et al., 2002) compared placebo pills to Saint-John's-wort (an herbal supplement, misleadingly promoted as a depression treatment) and Zoloft (sertraline, an SSRI) with 340 depressed individuals. "Full response" (e.g., recovery from depression) occurred in 31.9% of the placebo group, 23.9% in the Saint-John's-wort group, and just 24.8% of the Zoloft group. The average improvement with behavioral treatments is typically double or triple these placebo effects and the less effective drug and herbal effects. Since both the drug and herbal effects were even lower than the placebo response, it is misleading to say they have any "effect" in treating depression at all! Not surprisingly because Antonuccio's (1995) findings (and more recent findings) conclusively show that CBT, not drugs, most effectively treats depression, The researcher rightly has some serious concerns about drug therapy.

> I am concerned that physicians' continuing education training, most of which is paid for by pharmaceutical companies, will not adequately address contraindications for the use of tricyclic antidepressants.... I am concerned that patients, some of whom may not meet diagnostic criteria for depression, will be kept on medications indefinitely, despite the risks and despite the fact that safer, short-term, effective psychotherapeutic treatments are available. (p. 451)

Antonuccio follows these concerns to pinpoint what is behind this culture of drugging people:

> One may wonder why antidepressant medications continue to be the most common treatment for depression in the United States. At least part of the answer is effective marketing. Independent sources conservatively estimate that the $63 billion-a-year drug industry spends around $5 billion annually on drug promotion.... Unfortunately, one balanced scientific article on the efficacy of psychotherapy in the

American Psychologist is like a whimper in a stadium full of people cheering for drugs.... If good science alone were enough, psychotherapy would currently be the most prevalent treatment for depression instead of drug treatment. (1995, p. 451)

Good science dictates that when the evidence is clear that one approach is more effective than an alternative approach, it is important to know exactly why this is so. CBT is more effective than drugs in treating depression, therefore, it is important to know why.

WHAT MAKES CBT EFFECTIVE?

The behavioral components of CBT make it effective. Behavioral activation causes the changed cognitions that correlate to the alleviation of depression. Albert Ellis (1993) developed "rational emotive therapy," which was a "cognitive" therapy based on the assumption that irrational thoughts caused problems such as depression. But irrational thoughts are part of depression, not the cause of it. Ellis recognized that it was not sessions on the couch but the "behavioral homework" assignments given to depressed patients that both challenged their irrational cognitions ("Nobody likes me," "I'm not good at anything") and alleviated their depression. In 1993, Ellis changed the name of his therapy to "rational emotive *behavioral* therapy," acknowledging the causal status that behavioral activation had in effectively treating depression. By becoming active and learning new skills, depressed persons learn that people do like them and that they can do things. Consequently, their rate of reinforcement increases, and they feel productive, happy—better.

Similarly, Aaron Beck's (1975) cognitive theory and related therapy have been among the leading psychological approaches to treating depression for decades. But it turns out that much of the theory and treatment of cognitive psychology is unnecessary. What is necessary is behavioral activation. Research, led by psychologist Neil Jacobson, has found that behavioral activation is the critical component in effective "psychological" or "cognitive" treatment:

In a previous clinical trial, we found that so-called "cognitive" interventions were not necessary for the success of CT [cognitive therapy]: The behavioral activation (BA) component, a treatment precluding attempts to change thinking, worked as well as the entire CT package, both in maximizing acute treatment response and in relapse prevention over a two-year period.... The "cognitive" components of CT may not only be unnecessary but potentially a liability, since they result in a less parsimonious treatment package that may not be cost effective. (Jacobson & Gortner, 2000, p. 103)

Since drugs do not treat depression effectively, and much of cognitive therapy is unnecessary, it becomes important to define "antidepressant" and to make clear the answer.

WHAT IS AN "ANTIDEPRESSANT"?

Most people consider an "antidepressant" some sort of drug. Given the billions of dollars spent by the drug companies bombarding us with advertisements designed to convince us that depression is caused by a chemical imbalance in the brain, and that their drugs may "correct" this imbalance, it is not surprising that to most people "antidepressant" is synonymous with "drugs." But, as we saw earlier, this is *wrong*. Drugs are not antidepressants. Just as a drug addict may feel better while he or she is high on drugs, a person suffering from depression may feel better while on drugs too. However, because depression is *deactivated, depressed behavior*, this drug-induced "feeling better" does not address the real causes of depression. Instead, *behavioral activation*, resulting in *increases in response-contingent positive reinforcement*, is the most effective antidepressant. Becoming active, engaging in life, and receiving positive reinforcement for one's actions is the natural *lasting* antidepressant treatment. According to Neil S. Jacobson, Christopher Martell, and Sona Dimidjian (2001) of the University of Washington:

Behavioral activation (BA), [is] a stand-alone treatment for depression.... BA attempts to help depressed people reengage in their lives through focused activation strategies. These strategies counter patterns of avoidance, withdrawal, and inactivity that may exacerbate depressed episodes by generating additional secondary problems in individuals' lives. BA is designed to help individuals approach and access sources of positive reinforcement in their lives, which can serve a *natural antidepressant function*. (p. 255, italics added)

The natural antidepressant function of behavioral activation is completely logical and consistent with the behavioral understanding of depression "in which a decrease in pleasant events or an increase in aversive events was associated with the onset of depression. In this way, particular reinforcing qualities of a person's environment, such as low rates of positive reinforcement or increased rates of punishment, were assumed to be causally related to depression" (Jacobson et al., 2001, p. 256). This behavioral assumption was empirically verified in a study by University of Tennessee researchers, who used daily diaries of nondepressed and mildly depressed individuals to directly assess the behavioral claim that "depressed individuals receive less response-contingent positive reinforcement than non-depressed individuals, indicated by less engagement in behaviors perceived as rewarding in terms of both immediate pleasure and potential for these behaviors to result in more distal rewards" (Hopko, Armento, Cantu, Chambers, & Lejuez, 2003, p. 1137). These researchers found that depressed individuals

> engaged in significantly more behaviors perceived as unlikely to produce a future reward and significantly fewer behaviors perceived as likely to produce a future reward.... Depressed participants reported less reward subsequent to engaging in daily activities.... Depressed individuals rates themselves as more passive (p. 1142).... Consistent with previous findings and supportive of the behavioral model, results support the contention that a relationship exists between a lack of rewarding experiences and depressive symptoms. Self-reported depressive symptoms (and daily negative affective ratings) were inversely related to general activity level and the amount of reward or pleasure that participants obtained through interaction with the environment.... These findings are particularly provocative given the non-clinical, mildy depressed nature of the experimental group and one would expect a *magnification of already large effect sizes with inclusion of a clinically depressed sample....* [Furthermore] depressed individuals also reported a decreased expectation that current behaviors would result in a future reward. (p. 1144, italics added)

This study demonstrates that depression is caused by depressed behavior-environment interactions, *not* by a chemical imbalance in the brain.

Individuals with elevated depressive symptoms have not effectively identified and exposed themselves to positively reinforcing activities and events and therefore may be unaware of
more appealing alternative behaviors. Thus, although current
behaviors may not be considered overly pleasurable or likely
to produce much in the way of immediate or distal reward,
these behaviors may continue to be appealing relative to other
options (cf. McDowell, 1982) and although not positively
reinforced, may be maintained via other processes such as
negative reinforcement. For example, staying in bed might
not lead to career advancement or social rewards, but it might
allow the individual to avoid the less appealing alternatives in
their behavioral repertoire (e.g., working hard in class, spend-
ing time with a significant other that is demeaning). (Hopko
et al., 2003, p. 1145)

These behavioral difficulties are what behavioral activation directly
addresses and counters to work its antidepressant action. According to
Jacobson and Gortner (2000):

The behavior analytic framework emphasizes functional
analysis of the environmental events that have impinged on
individual clients to generate the depression, and formulates
cases in a way that looks outside [to casual behavior-environment interactions] rather than inside [to supposed chemical
imbalances or faulty thinking] the person for targeted change.
That is,...BA treatment conceptualizes depression in terms
of environmental events that have created contextual shifts,
which in turn have denied the client access to those reinforcers which normally functioned as anti-depressants. These
contextual shifts have to be corrected through targeted activation, activation aimed at altering the environment in such a
way that anti-depressant reinforcers are more easily
accessed....BA assumes that negative thinking is a realistic
by-product of stressful environments and that the thinking
will change automatically as reinforcers return to the client's
life. (pp. 112–113)

Unlike the drug approach, which assumes that depression has a simple
cause, "a chemical imbalance," and a simple one-size-fits-all treatment—

"take our drugs"—the behavioral understanding of depression recognizes the often complex and difficult lives that depressed people live and formulates treatment individualized to each person's unique life circumstances. Other than to increase the drug dosage, there is no individualized drug treatment. Furthermore, the behavioral understanding of depression can account "for the perpetuation of depressive behavior through avoidance of anti-depressant reinforcers: because contact with these potential reinforcers is often punishing in the short run, depressed people avoid contact, to their short-term relief but their long-term detriment. For example, a depressed man ... discovered that his wife had been unfaithful: this discovery triggered depressive behavior, including avoidance of interpersonal contact, contact which was ultimately necessary to provide access to anti-depressant reinforcers" (Jacobson & Gortner, 2000, p. 113).

In the aforementioned example, a "mental health professional" treating the depressed man with drugs may likely respond: "So your wife cheated on you. That must make you feel bad. Let's increase your dosage." The sources of this man's depression have not been addressed. He has simply been drugged.

Conversely, a therapist using the behavioral approach would recognize the man's avoidance of interpersonal contact, particularly with his wife, as a key causal and maintaining factor of his depression. In fact, depression is a "quite understandable response to life events, not an irrational response or one that is primarily a function of alterations in brain chemistry" (Jacobson & Gortner, 2000, p. 115). Rather than drugging the man, the behavioral therapist would likely design an individualized treatment that would include activating interpersonal contact. This activation might be initiated through such exercises as structured graduated homework exercises involving increasing rate and duration of interpersonal contacts, reciprocal behavioral contracting, journaling interpersonal interactions, and role-playing. Additionally, the man would be taught interpersonal skills designed to make his interactions more reinforcing for his wife, thus increasing his wife's rate of initiating interaction with her husband. Once these interpersonal behaviors have been activated, the new skills learned and assimilated into the man's behavioral repertoire, the natural antidepressant reinforcers that result from a stable, interactive, mutually loving marriage, and the reinforcers from other active interpersonal contacts will end the man's depression. While such an approach may not produce the immediate feel-good sensations that drugs can provide, the behavioral treatment is much more likely to result in long-term happiness.

Behavioral activation produces access to natural antidepressant reinforcers. One does not need to be on drugs for years, or for life, and often behavioral activation does not require extensive or complex therapy to be highly effective. Indeed, Derek Hopko and his colleagues developed *A Brief Behavioral Activation Treatment for Depression* (BATD), "based on the premise that increased activity (i.e., activation) and the resulting contact with positive consequences is sufficient for the reduction of depressive symptoms and the subsequent increase of positive thoughts and feelings" (Hopko, Lejuez, LePage, Hopko, & McNeil, 2003, p. 461). The treatment was tested in a psychiatric hospital with 25 severely depressed patients. The treatment included construction of an activity hierarchy with daily goals ranging from easy (e.g., making one's bed) to difficult (e.g., an interactive activity with another person for 1 hour). Additionally, "tokens were provided for the achievement of BATD-related goals. Tokens could be exchanged for off-unit ground passes, long-distance phone cards, snacks, or permission to participate in other activities" (p. 462). The tokens provided access to additional natural antidepressant reinforcers.

Patients receiving BATD had depression scores that decreased from 35.1 to 19.1 posttreatment, or 16 points on the Beck Depression Inventory. Conversely, the scores of patients receiving traditional supportive psychotherapy (the control group) only decreased from 37.1 to 30.2, just 7 points. "The difference between treatment groups was clinically meaningful, despite limited sample size" (p. 463). In addition to being more than twice that of the supportive psychotherapy group, the decrease in depression in the patients receiving BATD also was much greater than usually occurs with drug treatment (assuming that drugs produce any improvement at all). Not only is BATD more effective than standard psychotherapy and drugs, it also is more cost-effective. A depressed person may be kept on drugs for years, whereas the highly effective treatment in the Hopko and colleagues study lasted only 14 days, leading its authors to argue, "Given the limited time and training needed to implement this treatment, it appears ideal for inpatient settings in which managed care considerations have reduced the length of stay, thereby reducing the feasibility of more traditional interventions.... [BATD is] parsimonious and time-efficient" (pp. 463–464).

EXERCISE AND FRIENDSHIP

It turns out that even less-structured or traditional therapies can alleviate depression more effectively than can medication. The key factor in all of these approaches is that they cause behavioral activation resulting in access to natural antidepressant reinforcers. Perhaps the most effective and studied simple treatment for depression is nothing more than consistent, regular exercise.

Duke University Medical Center studied 156 patients over age 50 who had major depression. The patients were assigned to either Zoloft (sertraline) therapy, aerobic exercise, or a combination therapy of drugs and exercise. Four months after treatment began, all groups had shown improvement. However, 6 months after treatment, patients in the exercise group had lower relapse rates than the drugged patients. In patients who continued to exercise on their own the chance of relapse was even less (Babyak, Blumenthal, Herman, Khatri, Doraiswang, Moore, Craighead, Baldewicz, & Krishnan, 2000). Because of its very nature, exercise causes behavioral activation, which is a more effective antidepressant treatment than any SSRI or other supposed "antidepressant" drug. "It [exercise] helped me out a lot," said one senior citizen who used exercise to overcome depression caused by the death of her husband. "Now I don't have time to be depressed. I'm busy, busy all the time" (see Flora, 2004, p. 220). When a person's behavior is not depressed, the person is not "depressed."

Gregg Tkachuk and Garry Martin of the University of Manitoba, Canada, reviewed 14 studies on exercise and depression and found that regardless of the type of exercise (running, walking, or strength training just 20 to 60 minutes a day 3 times a week), those who exercised had significantly less depression. As long as exercise was maintained so was the improvement (Tkachuk & Martin, 1999). "Not only is exercise a viable treatment for mild to moderate [to severe (see Babyak et al., 2000)] depression," argues Tkachuk, "it is four to five times more cost-effective than traditional forms of psychotherapy." Not only does exercise in and of itself cause behavioral activation, it also puts people into contact with another powerful natural antidepressants—social reinforcement. "It gets people out in an environment where they receive positive reinforcement from others" (Tkachuk, 1999, p. 24).

A dearth of social reinforcement is a major cause of depression, the reason behavior becomes deactivated. In a study of 193 students in grades 3–6, it was found that "friendship networks...buffered [the children] from feelings of loneliness...and] loneliness proved to be the gateway through which the peer variables, particularly friendship, impacted depressed mood....Peer difficulties appeared to increase the risk of depression" (Nangle, Erdley, Newman, Mason, & Carpenter, 2003, pp. 551–552). In children, as in adults, depression is not caused by a chemical imbalance, but depression occurs because the child who is depressed does not receive, or have access to, sufficient behavior-contingent reinforcement, particularly social reinforcement. Drugging depressed children instead of ensuring that they receive sufficient behavior-contingent reinforcement is particularly unethical.

This relation between social reinforcement, the natural antidepressant, and depression holds *throughout the life span*. A Duke University study of predictors of depression outcome of older, depressed adults (age 60 or older) found that depressed, older adults with functional, instrumental activities in daily living and strong social support were more likely to have a positive outcome after 1 year. Similarly, a study of 90 patients with major depression in Madrid, Spain, found that patients who did not recover had less social support, smaller nonfamilial social networks, and less everyday support, leading the researchers to conclude that "satisfaction with social support was a good predictor of outcome independently of the severity and recurrence of depression" (Ezquiaga, Garcia, Pallores, & Bravo, 1999, pp. 214-215).

According to the "social causation model," a lack of social support, not a chemical imbalance in the brain, causes psychiatric symptoms, including depression. Robert Calsyn and Joel Winter of the University of Missouri-St. Louis examined the data of over 4,000 homeless individuals living in 18 cities and found that "natural support [support from family, relatives, coworkers, etc.] reduced psychotic symptoms at both 3 months and 12 months, supporting the social causation model" (2002, p. 254). For those very unfortunate people in the obviously depressing situation of homelessness, "natural support reduced both depression and psychotic symptoms" (p. 256). Again and again it is seen that, regardless of the cause of depression—the loss of a loved one, the unfaithfulness of a spouse, the lack of friends, or the depressing situation of homelessness—the more social support, the more social reinforcement, and the more natural antidepressant one receives, the more likely it is that one will recover from depression and the less likely it is that depression will occur in the first place.

If the lack of social support and friends is one of the major causes of depression, then it follows that increasing one's friendships should decrease depression. Time spent with a friend does in fact alleviate depression more effectively than any drug. British researcher Tirrill Harris assigned a "befriender" to depressed women who acted as a confidant for patients and met them for tea or other outings during the course of a year. After 1 year, 72% of patients who received the befriender treatment experienced recovery, whereas only 45% of the wait-list control patients recovered from depression (Harris, Brown, & Robinson, 1999).

Unfortunately, sufficient social support, sufficient social reinforcement, or the availability of a befriender simply does not exist for many sufferers of depression. Indeed, the lack of social support is in no small part the very cause of their depression. Fortunately, behavioral activation treatments directly build functional instrumental activities and social skills that result in improved social support. Once individuals become active and learn new social skills, their social support and social reinforcement increase, and their depression is alleviated. Given the *repeatedly* demonstrated superiority of behaviorally based treatments for depression, from cognitive behavioral therapy to behavioral activation to exercise to increasing friendships and socialization, and the *repeatedly* demonstrated ineffectiveness of drug-based treatments, treating people who suffer from depression with drugs as a first option (and possibly under any circumstances) is not only dishonest but unethical.

Chapter 8

Schizophrenia

Being told that a loved one has schizophrenia is one of the most devastating things a person can possibly hear. Schizophrenia is considered a psychotic disorder and is characterized by severe disturbances in thought (delusions) and perceptions (hallucinations). Without help, a person suffering from schizophrenia is unable to successfully function in life. A schizophrenic's hallucinations are almost always auditory, such as hearing voices that no one else can hear. The delusions may be of grandeur (e.g., believing that one is God) or persecution or of another paranoid type. For example, a person suffering from schizophrenia might believe that he is hearing voices originating from another planet, transmitted through a metal coat hanger telling him that although he is meant to rule the world, other aliens are sending radioactive death rays against him through car antennas that can only be blocked with metal trash can lids. The person fighting off the supposed death rays is picked up by the police as a "crazy person" waving trash can lids in the street. Although this example is fictional, the real problems of schizophrenia often are even more peculiar.

Unlike most of the other "disorders" listed in psychiatry's Diagnostic and Statistical Manual (DSM), which are creations of the psychiatric profession and pharmaceutical companies (Horwitz, 2002), schizophrenia has always been recognized as a legitimate, severe problem needing specialized treatment. Unfortunately, for much of human history, attempts to treat schizophrenia have been barbaric—insulin coma therapy, electroconvulsive shock therapy, lobotomy, exorcism, or worse. Improvements in the care and rehabilitation of people suffering from schizophrenia have generally been attributed to either improved pharmaceutical treatment or behavioral therapy, or a combination of the two. Although more effective drugs are frequently given credit for improved treatment for schizophrenia, a critical analysis reveals that behavioral programs deserve the vast majority of credit for any recovery or improvements in the lives of those suffering from schizophrenia. Critical analysis also reveals that although highly unusual, the problems schizophrenia sufferers are behavioral and are best treated as such.

PHARMACEUTICAL TREATMENT FOR SCHIZOPHRENIA

The discovery of chlorpromazine and other phenothiazine drugs in the 1950s is generally considered the first major medical advancement in the treatment of schizophrenia. Referred to as the "major tranquilizers," these drugs were somewhat successful in suppressing (tranquilizing) the behaviors of those suffering from schizophrenia and in turn making the patients easier to manage. But it is questionable at best if these drugs in any way improved people's lives. Many adverse side effects made compliance a major problem, and the people on the drugs, who compliantly shuffled from the day room to the cafeteria and back to the ward dorm, were said to do the "Thorazine shuffle." Thus the first drug "cure"—being tranquilized so that one shuffles around like a zombie and suffers from adverse side effects—may very well be worse than the disorder.

Supposed improvements in medication came with the development of the "neuroleptics" including the butyrophenons (haloperidol, a.k.a. "Haldol"). The new name for the drug class—neuroleptics—(meaning "to take hold of the nerves") also helped advance the illusion that psychiatry had nailed down the specific biological cause of, and cure for, schizophrenia. Is it a coincidence that the first four letters of the trade name are "halo"? Is one to make an implication that haloperidol was to make sufferers of schizophrenia angelic?

Although antidotes do not constitute scientific evidence, I can nevertheless testify that during graduate school, when I worked as a psychology aide and behavior specialist in a total institution for children and teenagers with severe problems, many, if not most, of the children were put on Haldol, Thorazine, or similar drugs, and the drugs did not help the children function or live better. Instead, if anything, they made the children easier to manage for the direct care staff. The drugs appeared to make the children more unhappy.

Corroborating my personal observations, research has found that these drugs do in fact increase unhappiness and have a host of unpleasant side effects. Although given a more modern label, "neuroleptics," they still basically function as tranquilizers. "Negative side effects are a major factor in patient refusal [to take medication]. Antipsychotics can produce a number of unwanted physical symptoms, such as grogginess, blurred vision, and dryness of the mouth" (Barlow & Durand, 2005, p. 479). The most modern drug, clozapine also has adverse side effects, including life-threatening ones (Umbricht & Kane, 1996). In addition to feeling constantly sedated, common side effects are the development of symptoms such as Parkinson's disease, parkinsonian symptoms, including akinesia, slow motor and speech behavior and an expressionless face, and tardive dyskinesia, uncontrollable movement and twitches of the face, often irreversible in up to 20% of patients (Morgenstern & Glazer, 1993). These side effects are a major reason 75% of patients reported refusing to take medication some time during treatment (Weiden, Dixion, Frances, Appelbaum, Haas, & Rapkin, 1991). If up to 75% of patients refuse drug treatment, then it becomes hard to argue that these medications are very helpful.

In *Medicating Schizophrenia: a History*, Sheldon Gelman (1999) shows that so-called advances in medicating schizophrenia in no way cured it or necessarily even improved sufferers' lives. The discovery of various medications for schizophrenia was not a result of a biological understanding of the problem or of a systematic research program. Instead, new medications were largely stumbled upon by accident. In an attempt to maintain the legitimacy of psychiatry as a medical profession, drug treatments for schizophrenia were advocated in spite of a lack of efficacy and in the face of many potential problems. After an exhaustive review of the research practices and history behind psychiatry's attempts to treat schizophrenia, Gelman concludes:

To the present day, theories about medication ignore inconvenient or negative inferences.... The identity, extent, and significance of other side effects [in addition to tardive dyskinesia]; the nature of medications' benefits; the implications of neurological changes; the relationship of research to public health and clinical prescribing—on all these matters, psychiatrist's conclusions zigzagged and reversed and inverted in an apparent effort to arrive at the most convenient results for the profession.... Psychiatry needs and claims progress, but the circumstances that give rise to the need—the last professional default—also refute the claims. (1999, pp. 226–229)

In short, despite claims to the contrary, drugging people who have schizophrenia is *not* an effective treatment.

BEHAVIORAL TREATMENT FOR SCHIZOPHRENIA

Behavioral treatments for schizophrenia make no claim to "cure" the problem. Instead, behavioral treatments empower people who have schizophrenia (Corrigan, 1997). "Behavioral interventions actually facilitate the decision-making abilities of many persons with severe psychiatric disorders" (Corrigan, 1997, p. 50). Behavioral treatments increase independence, social and vocational skills, quality of life, and happiness and reduce stress for both the family as well as the patient suffering from schizophrenia.

The basic token economy, so effective in improving many behavioral deficiencies (see the chapter on ADHD in this book and Flora, 2004, for reviews), is an effective tool in empowering persons with severe psychiatric disorders. Patrick Corrigan summarized the basic structure of token economies for persons suffering from schizophrenia:

First, a list of target behaviors is identified; these typically include social, coping, and self-care skills [and as these skills are remastered, work and other higher-level skills are incorporated]. Second, point contingencies are defined for each target behavior. The number of points for each behavior varies with the importance and difficulty of that behavior. For example, an "easy" behavior like brushing teeth receives 5 points, whereas a more "difficult" behavior like monitoring psychiatric warning signs receives 10 points. Finally, rules for cashing in points are defined. Typically, participants in a token economy exchange their points each day for a smorgasbord of commodities (e.g., hygiene products, snacks, stationery) and privileges (e.g., the Friday night pizza party). (1997, pp. 51–52)

There is nothing artificial about a token economy. I earn points—direct deposit pay into my bank account—first for dressing and engaging in self-hygiene behaviors and then by attending my committee meetings, teaching classes and performing other job duties. My points vary according to the difficulty of the task—more credit for graduate-level courses and less for freshman-level classes. If I miss classes, my points may be docked, or I may lose my job. Finally, I exchange my points (money) each day for a smorgasbord of commodities (e.g., hygiene products, snacks, stationery) and privileges (e.g., the Friday night pizza party). The token economy teaches basic social, work, and life functioning skills in which billions of humans worldwide must engage each day—important lessons for all. It is difficult to see how the pharmaceutical sedation of behavior contributes to such important learning.

In the first demonstration of the effectiveness of token economies in the care of schizophrenia, Gordon Paul and Robert Lentz found that patients in the token program did better on self-care, hygiene, and social and vocational skills and were more likely to be discharged from the psychiatric hospital (Paul & Lentz, 1977). Patrick Corrigan notes several beneficial effects of token economies for persons suffering from schizophrenia:

> First, they provide a safe and structured milieu for individuals to consider their options. Research has clearly shown that the rate of *chaos and aggression decreases significantly when token economies are instituted in the milieu* (Dickerson, Ringel, Parente, & Boronow, 1994; Paul & Lentz, 1977). The importance of a safe milieu should not be underestimated. Several studies have shown that many treatment programs are noisy and chaotic places that actually exacerbate agitation and psychotic symptoms (Drake & Sederer, 1986; Linn, Klett, & Caffey, 1980; Moos, 1974; Palmstierna, Huitfeldt, & Wistedt, 1991). . . . Second, token economies facilitate empowerment by clarifying options that a person may consider in a particular environment. Social exchange theorists argue that *all interpersonal interactions are governed by the exchange of rewards and punishers* (Kelley & Thibaut, 1978; LaValle, 1994; Molm, 1994). However, rules governing this exchange are frequently subtle such that persons with social cognitive deficits [people suffering from schizophrenia] are likely to miss them (Argyle, 1986; Trower, 1982). Token economies make explicit the contingencies in a social exchange [allowing the person who has schizophrenia to

make more informed autonomous choices]. (Corrigan, 1997, p. 52, italics added)

It would be a mistake to believe that behavioral treatment for schizophrenia is limited to token economies. Social skill training and behavioral family therapy are two additional standard parts of behavioral treatment for schizophrenia that greatly improve the lives of the patient and the patient's family. For a person suffering from delusions and hallucinations, it is difficult to make and maintain friendships and other social or intimate relationships. This inability to form and maintain relationships makes daily functioning more problematic and degrades the quality of one's life. Social skill training improves quality of life by teaching the psychotic patient how to build and maintain rewarding relationships.

In social skill training social skills are modeled and the patient rehearses and role-plays various social interactions. Interactions are broken down into their component parts, and the patient is encouraged and reinforced, verbally or with points in a token economy, for proper social behaviors. Patients may be given homework assignments to practice the newly acquired behaviors—standard behavioral treatment that is quite effective for a large range of difficulties. For people suffering from schizophrenia, "these learning activities have been used to teach basic conversation, assertiveness, symptom management, medication management, street smarts, and job readiness skills (Corrigan & Holms, 1994; Jacobs, Collier, & Wissusik, 1992; Liberman & Corrigan, 1993; Wallace, Liberman, MacKain, Blackwell, & Eckman, 1992)" (Corrigan, 1997, p. 52). As is the case with other problems, this behavioral social skill training greatly improves the quality of life for those suffering from schizophrenia. Although relapses may still occur, this training reduces both relapses and negative symptoms (Dobson, McDougall, Busheikin, & Aldons, 1995).

In behavioral family training, often resembling classroom education, family members are taught about schizophrenia, side effects of the medications the patient may be taking, problem-solving strategies, and communication skills—more effective and constructive ways to interact with the family member who suffers with schizophrenia. This is important, because "some family members dealing with the financial and emotional burden of a loved one's mental illness may unintentionally exacerbate psychotic symptoms with their angry and hostile reactions to the person (Coyne, Kessler, Tal, Trumbull, Wortman, & Greden, 1987; Jackson, Smith, & McCorry, 1990)" (Corrigan, 1997, p. 54). Additionally, such training significantly improves the lives of the entire family and the functioning and well-being of the person who has schizophrenia (Hogarty, Anderson, Reiss, Komblith, Greenwald, Ulrich, & Carter, 1991). Social skill training and behavioral family training greatly avoid or delay relapses of schizophrenic episodes (Falloon, Brooker, & Graham-Hole, 1992).

Rather than "control" or manipulate persons with severe mental illness as those who misconstrue or caricature behavioral treatment argue, behavioral treatment increases behavioral freedom, autonomy, and the quality of life for the person suffering from mental illness (see Flora, 2004), as Patrick Corrigan astutely observes:

> Behavior therapy clearly seems to empower persons with severe mental illness. Contrary to concerns of the phenomenologists, behavioral interventions do not control people, they help people to better control their environments. Token economies help to provide a safe place for persons to consider their life decisions. Token economies also clarify the range of choices that comprise many of these decisions. Skills training and cognitive rehabilitation teach persons with severe mental illness the skills necessary to meet the demands of independent decision making and community living. Behavior family therapy teaches family members skills so that they can provide more resources to persons with severe mental illness. Persons with these resources are better able to live independently. Finally, self-management techniques give persons more control over their behaviors and the settings in which they occur. *Behavior therapy facilitates empowerment.* (Corrigan, 1997, p. 56, italics added)

WHERE DO HALLUCINATIONS COME FROM, AND WHAT ARE THEY?

The voices that many schizophrenia sufferers claim to hear must come from somewhere. They do not come from outer space, Satan, or a deity. Instead, most likely the person is talking to himself or herself, but for some reason he or she does not recognize the source of this covert verbal behavior. Supporting this conclusion are brain imaging studies that reveal the area responsible for speech production (Broca's area) becomes more active during hallucinations, but the area for speech comprehension (Wernicke's area) does not become more active (Cleghorn, Franco, Szachtman, Kaplan, Szechtman, Brown, Nahmias & Garnett, 1992; McGuire, Shah, & Murray, 1993). These results are consistent with those that one would obtain if one were to take brain images of normal subjects who were asked to talk silently to themselves. Apparently, people suffering from hallucinations are actually talking silently to themselves as well.

Since psychotic behaviors are behaviors, unusual behaviors, perhaps, but behaviors nevertheless, they should respond like other behaviors when basic behavioral modification procedures are applied, and they do. In one case study, the appropriate speech of an adult diagnosed with chronic schizophrenia was reinforced with eye contact and therapist responses (positive reinforcement of appropriate behavior), and when the patient uttered bizarre comments the therapist would look away and not respond for 10 seconds (extinction of psychotic behavior). This procedure resulted in significant increases in appropriate vocalizations and decreases in bizarre verbalizations. Similarly, Liberman, Teigne, Patterson, and Baker (1973) reinforced appropriate conversations in schizophrenia patients who had been hospitalized for an average of 17 years. Normal informal conversations during evening relaxation with a nurse-therapist were reinforced with conversation, coffee, snacks, and cigarettes. Patients earned this relaxing time by conversing normally during daytime interviews. If patients spoke in a delusional fashion, then the interviews were ended. Rational speech increased from 200% to 600%, and correspondingly, delusional speech decreased.

Of course, decreasing overt delusional verbal behavior does not necessarily mean that the patient's covert (talking silently to oneself) delusional speech has diminished. More modern behavioral approaches recognize this possibility. Instead of trying to sedate delusions away with medication, modern behavioral approaches teach patients to accept that they may have delusional thoughts and to recognize them as such, rather than dwell on them, which reinforces the persistence and strength of the delusions.

Since the hallucinations are one's own covert verbal behavior, recognizing this should reduce psychotic problems—and it does. When patients are taught that stressful life events may cause misinterpretation of events and even delusions and hallucinations, are asked whether their symptoms are associated with stress, and are asked to consider whether the "voices" may be of their own making, the patients improve (Brenner, Hodel, Roder, & Corrigan, 1992; Kingdon & Turkington, 1991; McNally & Goldberg, 1997). While no claim is made that this procedure "cures" schizophrenia, it does help individuals understand that their symptoms may be a natural response to stress. This understanding then allows a shift from focusing on the symptoms—the delusions—to enabling them to focus on addressing the stressful environments or dysfunctional life situations that precede the symptoms.

Recent groundbreaking work in behavioral acceptance and commitment therapy (ACT) supports and strengthens this position. In the first study of ACT for schizophrenia, in only four sessions participants were taught

> to accept unavoidable private events [such as hallucinations and delusions]; to identify and focus on actions [behaviors] directed toward valued goals [reinforcers]; and to defuse from odd cognition, just noticing thoughts rather than treating them as either true or false. [Compared to treatment as usual (TAU),] ACT participants showed significantly higher symptom reporting and lower symptom believability and a rate of rehospitalization half that of TAU participants over a 4-month follow-up period. (Bach & Hayes, 2002, p. 1129)

Perhaps because the ACT patients learned to accept their private behaviors as a natural occurrence rather than as something that must be avoided and to focus on what they valued in life, "Participants on the ACT condition were considerably more likely to report symptoms than were TAU participants, and they were three times more likely to stay out of the hospital if they did" (Bach & Hayes, 2002, p. 1135). Similar to people with obsessive-compulsive problems, the more people who have schizophrenia attempt to avoid disturbing thoughts the more they occur, and the more emotionally and behaviorally destructive they become. Exposure to, and acceptance of, the difficulty may be necessary to move on. This is the basic approach in ACT, whether the problem is obsessions or psychotic symptoms: "ACT therapists try to help clients make room for...life's difficulties [even hallucinations] and to move in the direction of their chosen values. The barriers to doing this are experiential avoidance and cognitive fusion, which prevent a behavioral commitment to living a valued life" (Hayes, Strosahl, & Wilson, 1999, p. 81).

A more recent ACT study on schizophrenia, where "patients were encouraged to increase their willingness to accept the *experience* of psychotic symptoms non-judgmentally, while practicing valued behavioral goals" (Gaudiano & Herbert, 2006, p. 422, italics in orginal), found similar results: "At 4-month follow-up, 45% [9 of 20] of participants in the ETAU [enhanced treatment as usual] only condition were rehospitalized compared to only 28% [5 of 18] of those in the ACT condition" (Gaudiano & Herbert, 2006, p. 428). Additionally "the ACT group showed superiority to ETAU on measures related to affective severity, global improvement, distress associated with hallucinations, and social functioning. Furthermore, the ACT group demonstrated greater overall clinically significant symptom improvement" (Gaudiano & Herbert, 2006, p. 430).

The more attention psychotic symptoms are given, the more likely they are to be reinforced and actually strengthened. A healthier approach may be to simply acknowledge their existence and then move on.

Like other behavioral treatment approaches to schizophrenia, ACT behavioral treatments for schizophrenia make no attempt to "cure" the problem. Instead, ACT and other behavioral treatments empower people who have schizophrenia. Drug treatment fosters helplessness, the idea that unusual thoughts or perceptions are unacceptable, and that a normal, valued life is not possible while such thoughts or perceptions occur. Behavioral approaches, on the other hand, help people accept life's inevitable limitations and barriers and then move toward valued and reinforcing life goals.

A BIOLOGICAL COMPARISON

Of course the pharmaceutical approach to schizophrenia works by altering the body's chemistry, more specifically the body's brain chemistry. Although these drugs are given to many people, science (psychologists and psychiatrists) is ignorant of just how these drugs work: "We are just beginning to understand the mechanisms by which these drugs work" (Barlow & Durand 2005, p. 479). Yet it *is* known which neurotransmitter system these drugs affect: "The neuroleptics are dopamine antagonists. One of their major actions in the brain is to interfere with the dopamine neurotransmitter system" (Barlow & Durand 2005, p. 478). That is, drugs given to people suffering from schizophrenia will alter (reduce), the brain's dopamine activity.

This is important, because it is known that dopamine is the primary neurotransmitter involved in the reinforcement process and in the feeling of reward and pleasure (see Flora, 2004, p. 161). Additionally, "Dopamine activity is associated with exploratory, outgoing, pleasure-seeking behaviors" (Barlow & Durand, 2005, p. 50). Therefore, giving people who suffer from schizophrenia neuroleptics may make them more manageable, as the suppressed dopamine activity will make them less exploratory and outgoing. It also will reduce their ability to seek pleasure, to feel rewarded. Reinforcing activities will be engaged in less, as the activities will become less reinforcing because of the chemically induced reduced dopamine activity. Therefore, another reason medication refusal is so common may be that patients are simply tired of being made to feel unhappy by dopamine antagonist drugs, and so they refuse medication in an attempt to again feel some pleasure in their lives. Giving people who are suffering from schizophrenia neuroleptics may very well reduce the quality and value of their life and the experience of pleasure. This hardly seems humane.

Conversely, as described earlier, the behavioral approach helps persons suffering from schizophrenia gain more reinforcers, experience a more valued life, and feel more pleasure in life by empowering them with functional life skills. When a person (who is not on neuroleptics) feels pleasure or gains reinforcers, her or his dopamine level will spike. But as dopamine antagonists, the neuroleptics may prevent or suppress this spike, thus preventing the feeling of pleasure or reinforcement. With a drug-induced, diminished capacity to feel pleasure, the drug "cure" for schizophrenia may be a cruel cure indeed.

Chapter 9

Health Concerns, Head to Toe

SLEEP'S SEDUCTION

The "news" of March 29, 2005, was something that most Americans knew already—many Americans are not getting enough sleep. But what made the known *news* was that according to the National Sleep Foundation the problem had reached epidemic proportions. One in 6 Americans was getting less than 6 hours of sleep a night, a 33% increase since the foundation's first report in 1998. Furthermore, these sleep problems led to other problems, as 30% reported that sleep deprivation contributed to relationship problems, and 20% reported less sex as a result. Despite these problems, 70% of respondents did not talk to their doctors about their sleep difficulties (Zwillich, 2005a).

But there was no need to worry for these sleepy souls. The very evening newscasts that announced the sleeplessness epidemic were supported by frequent advertisements for Ambiem, a sleeping pill! How convenient—too convenient. The National Sleep Foundation is not funded by a bunch of sleepy sufferers who organized to fight for their right to sleep through the night. No, the foundation is funded by the makers of sleeping pills.

A sleep research finding more newsworthy than the foundation's self-serving survey had appeared less than 1 year earlier. But because the results could not be used to turn profits, that finding was not promoted. In "Cognitive Behavior Therapy [CBT] and Pharmacotherapy for Insomnia," Gregg Jacobs, PhD and coresearchers from the Sleep Disorders Center of the Beth Israel Medical Center and Harvard

Medical School directly compared Ambiem to CBT for the treatment of chronic insomnia. The results of the comparison were clear and telling:

> CBT was the most sleep effective intervention; it produced the greatest changes in sleep-onset latency and sleep efficiency, yielded the largest number of normal sleepers after treatment, and maintained therapeutic gains at long-term follow-up. The combined treatment provided no advantage over CBT alone, whereas pharmacotherapy produced only moderate improvements during drug administration and returned measures toward baseline after drug use discontinuation.... These findings sugggest that young and middle-age patients with sleep-onset insomnia can derive significantly greater benefit from CBT than pharmacotherapy and that CBT should be considered a first-line intervention for chronic insomnia. Increased recognition of the efficacy of CBT and more widespread recommendations for its use could improve the quality of life of a large number of patients with insomnia. (Jacobs, Pace-Schott, Stickgold, & Otto, 2004, 1888)

Patients in the CBT group had a 44% reduction in the time it took to fall asleep. The drugged patients had only a 29% reduction, which was lost when medication was discontinued. According to Jacobs, "Sleeping pills are the most frequent treatment for insomnia, yet CBT techniques clearly were more successful in helping the majority of study participants to become normal sleepers. The pills were found to be only moderately effective compared with CBT, and lost their effectiveness soon after they were discontinued" (quoted in Rosack, 2004, p. 32).

Not surprisingly, then, the outcome of comparing the drug approach to the behavioral approach for the treatment of insomnia is the same outcome of *every other* comparison between drugs and behavioral therapy for behavioral problems—people derive *significantly greater benefits* from the behavioral approach, the behavioral approach should be considered a *first-line intervention*, and *more widespread recommendations for its use could improve the quality of life* for many.

But, as with other problems, it is easier to pop a sleeping pill than it is to go through CBT. For insomnia, CBT's key component is simple "sleep hygiene." Sleep hygiene includes such basic life changes as regular exercise not closer than 6 hours before bed; being in bed for only sleeping and sex; getting out of bed if one does not fall asleep in about a half hour and performing an activity such as reading or crossword puzzles and returning to bed only when sleepiness returns; not checking the clock while in bed, and even removing it from the bedroom (people with sleep problems often spend more time checking the clock and worrying about sleep loss than they spend sleeping); getting out of bed at the same time every day, regardless of what time one goes to sleep; and not napping, or limiting naps to early in the day for 1 hour or less. People who have sleep problems often take long naps to "catch up" from lost sleep the previous night, but in fact the long-term result of late-day napping is that the napper is not tired and ready to sleep at night, creating a downward spiral of sleep difficulties. While it is simple to list behaviors involved in good sleep hygiene, changing one's life patterns can be difficult, and many may prefer powerful drugs to good sleep hygiene, despite the drug's adverse side effects (side effects that one may be given additional prescriptions to control). Although drugging may be easier, for those with real sleep problems who are serious about getting lasting, effective help and living happier and healthier lives, the behavioral treatment is clearly superior to popping sleeping pills.

JUST GET OUT OF THE BEDROOM! ERECTILE DYSFUNCTION AND PREMATURE EJACULATION

Apparently, no place and no behavior are safe from the profit-hungry drug companies. At the time of this writing, Johnson & Johnson is using the following well-worn strategy: (1) create a problem, (2) hype it, (3) get it noticed, (4) push a money-making drug to treat it, and (5) laugh all the way to the bank. In this case, it is the problem of premature ejaculation. Simple nondrug procedures already exist that can safely, easily, reliably, and often *enjoyably* treat premature ejaculation without drugs.

Of course, the makers of Viagra, Levitra, and Cialis have already successfully used this approach for erectile "dysfunction" (ED). *Never getting an erection* is infrequently a medical problem. Most of the time it is due to enormous life stressors or the result of taking drugs, legal or illegal. The ED drugs are not meant for these situations, as they may not work or may be contraindicated. In fact, the actual number of people who have real ED problems is so small that using ED drugs for them would not be profitable.

It is the *natural, normal,* but perhaps unwanted, decrease in frequency, duration, and rigidity of erections that occurs in all aging males that is targeted by the ED drug advertisements. It is a fact of life that as males age they produce less testosterone and have other normal, age-related declines in sexually related processes. Getting older is not a disease that requires drugs. A teenage boy may get an erection simply by looking at his teacher. Later, he may get an erection by talking with his girlfriend on the phone. Still later in life he may not achieve an erection until he is engaged in kissing and fondling. Even still later in life the same male may now require vigorous direct manipulation of the penis in order to achieve an erection, and even then he may only be able to achieve an erection once a week or less. However, this man has not developed a disease that requires drugging. He has simply grown older.

In addition to a natural decrease in erections with age, obesity and lack of exercise also contribute to erectile decline in men. As reported in the *Journal of the American Medical Association* (JAMA), a team of Italian MD researchers studied the effect of lifestyle changes on erectile dysfunction in 110 obese men and found that

> lifestyle changes, including reduced calorie diet and increased exercise, improve erectile function in obese men and resulted in about one third of men with erectile dysfunction regaining sexual function after treatment. This improvement was associated with amelioration of both endothelial function and markers of systemic vascular inflammation. Interventions focused on modifiable health behaviors may represent a safe strategy to improve erectile function and reduce cardiovascular risk in obese patients. (Esposito, Giugliano, DiPalo, Giugliano, Marfella, D'Andrea, D'Armieato, & Giugliano, 2004, p. 2983)

Obese or not, according to *Scientific American,* specific exercises targeting the pelvic musculature are more effective than Viagra: "A recently published study by urologist Frank Sommers of the University Medical Center in Cologne, Germany, showed that regular targeted exercise improved the sexual potency of 80 percent of the men who tried it, compared with 74 percent of men treated with Viagra" (Schmidt, 2005, p. 91).

Furthermore, when taking Viagra, vessels in the eyes are affected, in addition to vessels in the penis. According to claims by some patients, the drug may have caused partial or complete blindness.

Although the drug makers have denied a connection, on July 8, 2005, the FDA ordered the makers of Viagra, Cialis, and Levitra to include label information about cases of blindness. The FDA's alert read in part: "Men have lost eyesight in one eye some time after taking Viagra, Cialis, or Levitra. This type of vision loss is called non-arteritic anterior ischemic optic neuropathy (NAION). NAION causes sudden loss of eyesight because blood flow is blocked to the optic nerve. . . . Stop using Viagra, Cialis, or Levritra if you have a loss of eyesight. Get medical help right away."

With patients claiming Viagra is causing blindness, the comparison of the drug approach to the behavioral approach to increase erections turns out to be just another specific example of the general finding that the drug approach is little more, if anything, than a chemical whitewash with adverse side effects, in this case, possible blindness. Conversely, the behavioral approach (exercise) is more effective, with beneficial side effects—in this case, improved health and reduced cardiovascular risk. If a man chooses to take an ED drug, then he has been "taken" by the drug companies and has bought into the philosophy of "better living through chemistry," originally pushed by Timothy Leary to advocate LSD use. For the vast majority of ED drug takers, the accurate name is "age-related erectile *decline*," or "obesity-related *decline*," not "dysfunction"— nothing is "*dis*functioning," it is just functioning less.

Premature Ejaculation

Just as it is a misnomer to call a decrease in erections a dysfunction, it also is a misnomer to call premature ejaculation a dysfunction. Technically speaking, in terms of natural selection, an ejaculation is premature only if it occurs prior to the penis penetrating the vagina. In fact, ejaculation immediately after penetration is the *most* adaptive time to ejaculate. During the course of evolution, an animal, including the human animal, is highly vulnerable to attack from a rival male or by a predator during intercourse. Therefore, rapid copulation is a more adaptive strategy than protracted copulation. Over the course of natural history, those that quickly ejaculated would be at a selective advantage over those organisms that took their time. "Premature" ejaculation may have an evolutionary basis.

But it also could be argued that over the course of natural history, those organisms that found sex relatively more pleasurable, more reinforcing, would tend to seek it out and engage in sex more frequently than those that experienced sex as less reinforcing. Thus to the extent that fast ejaculation decreased the reinforcing value of sex, those organisms that ejaculated quickly would be at a selective disadvantage.

Regardless of which evolutionary perspective is correct, time to ejaculation and frequency of ejaculation are positively correlated to the level of male sex hormones, which is why teenagers and young men most commonly "suffer" from "premature" ejaculation—their male hormones are at their lifetime peak. But the major reason men ejaculate sooner than either they desire or their partners desire is because through masturbation, *men teach themselves, condition themselves, to ejaculate quickly.*

Virtually every human male begins to masturbate sometime during adolescence, but his natural, normal activity may be embarrassing. In many cases, there are family, social, and religious taboos against masturbating, even if masturbation occurs in private. When masturbating, the male will attempt to reach orgasm as quickly as possible to avoid the punishment associated with this natural activity. In other cases, in private, away from parental or other authorities, adolescent male friends may masturbate together, and the "winner" is the boy who ejaculates first. By the time a male has his first sexual intercourse with a female, he has masturbated hundreds, if not thousands, of times, and each time he has attempted to ejaculate as quickly as possible. In addition to high levels of hormones that predispose quick ejaculation, the male has conditioned himself, taught himself, to ejaculate "prematurely." Fast ejaculation is a *learned function.*

Just as speed of ejaculation is a learned function, more delayed ejaculation can be learned as well. Disseminating this knowledge produces no profits for shareholders, but a patented drug to "treat" the "dysfunction" of premature ejaculation may bring hundreds of millions of dollars of profit. In a promotional slight-of-hand with a press release by Otho-McNeil (a Johnson & Johnson pharmaceutical company), the learned behavior of premature ejaculation became a "medical condition" treated with drugs: "'Premature ejaculation is a frequent and distinct medical condition that can severely impact quality of life, affecting the physical and emotional well-being of patients and their partners,' says James H. Barada, MD, urologist at the Center for Male Sexual Health, Albany, New York, and board member of the Sexual Medicine Society of North America (SMSNA)" (Otho-McNeil, 2004). Toward the end of the release it was acknowledged that "Johnson & Johnson Pharmaceutical Research & Development supported the SMSNA Scientific Working

Group." One conclusion from this acknowledgment is that SMSNA is not a scientific organization releasing unbiased research for public consumption. It is simply a cover for a profit-hungry drug company.

The ball meant to snowball into drug company profits really started rolling with a study published in the *Journal of Sexual Medicine* (Patrick et al., 2005) and widely covered in the popular press. This study helped *create* the medical problem. The researchers reported that "premature ejaculation (PE) is the most common male sexual dysfunction, affecting approximately 20 percent to 30 percent of the male population at any one time" (CNN.com, 2005). The press hyped the report and the perceived lack of treatment, quoting researchers: "Currently, available data suggest that only 1 percent to 12 percent of males self-reporting PE receive treatment for their dysfunction" (CNN.com, 2005). But this study was not motivated by clinical psychology researchers eager to get to the bottom of a sexual dysfunction epidemic. Why would they be? If there was a real sexual dysfunction epidemic, meaning that sex behaviors were dysfunctioning at the level of a population epidemic, then the very survival of the human species would be in peril. There is no epidemic. Information on the causes and effective nondrug treatments for PE is widely available. No, just like the SMSNA, "The study was funded in part by Mountian View, California-based, Alza Corp. and Johnson & Johnson Pharmaceutical Services, LLC, which are seeking Food and Drug Administration approval for the drug Dapoxetine for treating premature ejaculation." Surprise, surprise.

Of course, Johnson & Johnson is more than willing to come to the rescue of all the men who are supposedly suffering from this "dysfunction" with their drug. *Red Herring: The Business of Technology* reported on its Web site, "Johnson & Johnson announces *successful pivotal trial* results for a drug to treat premature ejaculation" (Red Herring, 2005, italics). Note that this is not from a medical, psychological, or science Web site but a business Web site. While reporting that Johnson & Johnson claimed that the drug "can increase the length of intercourse by three or four times.... [Additionally] scientists and physicians at the centenary annual meeting of the American Urology Association heard that the drug known as dapoxetine hydrochloride increased control, satisfaction, and sexual function," Johnson & Johnson's rising stock price also was noted.

Misinformation, not fact, was presented as well: "'There are no truly optimal therapies for PE,'" Jon Pryor, lead investigator on the trial, said at the Monday meeting" (Red Herring, 2005). This claim may be true with regard to drug "treatments," but it is false when simple behavioral approaches are considered. This misinformation is promoted for profit. The report notes that Goldman Sachs analysts believe that the profit for the drug will be $100 million in 2007, when it will arrive on the market.

Men do not need drugs for successful, mutually enjoyable sexual intercourse. They have been doing it since existence. Rather than taking drugs to delay ejaculation or the popularly portrayed tactic of reciting baseball batting averages to delay ejaculation during intercourse, the behavioral treatments are enjoyable and effective, and several can increase the intimacy of the sex act.

While not increasing intimacy, an effective, and likely enjoyable, method to delay ejaculation during intercourse is for the male to masturbate earlier in the day. As a result of the natural cycle of sexual arousal/plateau/orgasm/resolution, a recent orgasm will delay the current orgasm. For a particularly rapidly cycling male, his partner could even masturbate him to orgasm early in the sexual encounter, which would be followed by more delayed ejaculation during intercourse. Most men would prefer to have two naturally stimulated orgasms over one orgasm artificially delayed by drugs.

With the publication of *Human Sexual Inadequacy* by William Masters and Virginia Johnson in 1970, the effective behavioral approach to treating sexual problems became available to anyone who was willing to read. While the drug companies are promoting drugs that many men will take covertly, the basis for treatment for all problems in Masters and Johnson's approach is *communication* between partners. Once partners are openly communicating about their sexual desires and sexual functioning, men can learn to delay ejaculation in the context of a loving relationship, without drugs.

One effective nondrug method is the squeeze technique. When the male reaches plateau during intercourse, the penis is withdrawn and either the male or his partner squeezes the head of the penis. This causes a decrease in arousal at which time intercourse is resumed. Over several sessions this practice is repeated and the duration of intercourse is increased. The result is that the man will learn to control his orgasms. The squeeze technique also can be practiced during masturbation, as can several other exercises (e.g., pelvic floor exercises, similar to stopping urination in midflow) that teach more controlled, delayed ejaculations.

Masters and Johnson taught their clients to first learn and use nongenital pleasuring. Nongenital pleasuring allows partners to learn to enjoy each other physically without "performance anxiety" that may result in either an inability to achieve an erection or in premature ejaculation. Only after nongenital pleasuring occurred was genital pleasuring attempted. This would be followed by gradual, partial insertion of the penis, and gradually followed, over several sessions, by deeper penetration and increased trust. This approach resulted in the resolution of premature ejaculation in close to 100% of their clients.

The purpose here is not to present sexually explicit information for its own sake, but to show that basic behavioral learning techniques can remedy the behavioral problem of premature ejaculation nearly 100% of the time. But the drug companies are positioning this behavioral problem as a "medical disorder" requiring drugs—drugs that produce the side effects nausea, loss of appetite, and, ironically, loss of sexual desire. When a completely effective nondrug treatment already exists, the ethics of all involved in the promotion of the drug treatment must be questioned.

MORE TROUBLE BELOW: IRRITABLE BOWEL SYNDROME, PREMENSTRUAL SYNDROME, AND URINARY INCONTINENCE

Irritable bowel syndrome (IBS) and urinary incontinence (UI) both involve basic biological processes, and at first glance they may appear to be problems of physiology best treated medically. However, both IBS and UI are best viewed as behavioral difficulties, and the evidence is quite conclusive that behavioral treatments are more effective (and lack adverse side effects) compared to drug treatments.

People suffering from IBS have severe abdominal pain, cramping, or tenderness and alternating bowel movements: either diarrhea, constipation, or constipation and diarrhea not caused by other gastrointestinal diseases or disorders. IBS sufferers usually are experiencing distress (e.g., Blanchard & Malamood, 1996), anxiety and or depression that may or may not be acknowledged (e.g., Tirch & Radnitz, 1997).

Having an irritable bowel in response to stressful events is *normal*. In response to a stressor, the sympathetic division of the autonomic nervous system initiates several biological functions, including stimulating the adrenal gland and shutting down the digestive system. Professional and amateur performers and athletes (as well as the author) regularly experience irritable bowels prior to an event. Loose stools, frequent urination, stomach upset, and vomiting are all common. The body shuts down its energy-consuming digestive processes and attempts to empty its digestive tract so that maximum physiological resources are available to deal with the stressor. Nonperformers and athletes also may experience an irritable bowel prior to and during other stressful events, such as the impending visit of a difficult relative. This digestive shutdown is an evolutionary adaptation, as those whose digestive processes shut down when encountering environmental emergencies would be at a selective advantage over those who continued to use physiological resources to digest food during an emergency. While an irritable bowel may be unpleasant, it is normal, not a disease, disorder, or dysfunction.

The problem for the IBS sufferer is that the irritable bowel is chronic and appears not to be in response to easily identifiable stressors. Since the condition appears to be chronic, many falsely conclude that it must be a medical condition. But the condition is psychological, behavioral, a response to stressors, anxiety and/or depression. A study of 188 IBS sufferers, "Psychopathology in Irritable Bowel Syndrome: Support for a Psychophysiological Model," (Sykes, Blanchard, Lackner, Keefer, & Krasner, 2003), found that "overall, these results support the idea that IBS is a psychophysiological disorder, . . . that IBS patients report a high level of psychopathology, . . . [and that] it appears that psychological factors may be involved in both the onset and maintenance of GI symptoms" (pp. 369–371). That is, the researchers found that psychological problems cause the symptoms of IBS, not vice versa. It logically follows that if the condition is in fact a manifestation of chronic anxiety, then teaching sufferers to relax should reduce IBS. It does.

When IBS sufferers were taught and practiced a simple relaxation response meditation program that consisted of "selecting a quiet environment, assuming a comfortable position, focusing on the word 'one,' and maintaining a passive attitude" (Keefer & Blanchard, 2001, p. 805), all sufferers experienced a reduction in symptoms and at 3-month follow-up "25% of patients had maintained their initial treatment gains, with no additional improvement, 52% of patients had once again improved their symptoms from post-treatment. . . . There were significant reductions in flatulence, belching, bloating, and diarrhea" (Keefer & Blanchard, 2001, p. 808).

Compared to drug treatment, which often results in adverse side effects, the study, which was conducted at the Center for Stress and Anxiety Disorders, University at Albany, New York, found beneficial side effects of the relaxation response meditation program. Not only did "the meditation treatment [lead] to significant immediate relief from problems caused by flatulence and belching, and to . . . reductions in diarrhea, constipation, and bloating," but also "the meditation appeared to be helpful in alleviating conditions other than gastrointestinal distress, including headache, insomnia, hypertension, backache, worry, depression, anxiety, and jumpiness, as well as subjectively increasing energy, enjoyment in life, and concentration. This is important as collateral effects of this treatment may improve overall quality of life" (Keefer & Blanchard, 2001, p. 809). Collateral effects of drugs are usually aversive, but when people are taught a simple, straightforward, behavioral approach to relaxation that they can control, not only are IBS symptoms reduced or eliminated, but patients' entire lives may change for the better. "One patient reported that she was finally able to sleep and that she had no more diarrhea. She was also doing very well in her new job. A second patient reported that she no longer needed to take her anti-hypertension medication, and that her blood pressure had returned to normal. . . . A third patient left her very stressful job and began her own business" (Keefer & Blanchard, 2001, p. 808).

The drugs that are meant to target IBS are particularly dangerous. One drug, Lotronex, resulted in at least 70 severe reactions, including five deaths. The FDA removed the drug in November 2000. It is again available, but patients must sign a patient-physician agreement before receiving a prescription. Other drugs given to "treat" IBS include anti-depressants and our old friends the SSRIs, such as Paxil (e.g., DeNoon, 2004). Using the SSRIs for IBS is just treating a new problem with more of the familiar chemical brain whitewash drugs that have the same side effects.

Not only is psychotherapy more effective than Paxil (paroxetine), it is more cost-effective. British researchers compared the cost-effectiveness of psychotherapy (only eight sessions) and paroxetine (20 mg of Paxil daily) for severe IBS and found that "During the follow-up year, psychotherapy but not paroxetine was associated with a significant reduction in health care costs compared with treatment as usual" (Creed, Fernandes, Guthrie, Palmer, Ratcliffe, Reed, Rigby, Thompson, & Tomenson, 2003, p. 303).

If services can be effectively delivered to a group of patients, then such therapy is more cost-effective than individual therapy, and even more cost-effective compared to drugs. A team of Canadian researchers found that cognitive-behavioral group therapy (CBGT) can effectively reduce IBS symptoms and improve quality of life in IBS sufferers

(Tkachuk, Graff, Martin, & Bernstein, 2003). First they noted the differences in the effectiveness of drugs compared to CBGT:

> Historically, standard medical treatment, consisting of trials of bulking agents, antispasmodics, motility agents, and tricyclic antidepressants, has been minimally effective (Klein, 1988). Recent attempts to develop safe, effective medications (e.g., 5TH3 antagonists [Paxil is one such antagonist]) have also been problematic. Individualized cognitive-behavioral therapy, targeting symptom reduction and improved daily functioning, has emerged as an empirically supported treatment option (Compas, Haaga, Keefe, Leitenberg, & Williams, 1998). (Tkachuk et al., 2003, p. 58)

In the study, patients receiving CBGT received 10, 90-minute group sessions over 9 weeks. The CBGT consisted of patient education and goal setting, relaxation training, cognitive therapy, assertion training, and relapse prevention strategies, where "patients reviewed acquired coping skills, identified future high-risk stress-producing situations, and prepared coping alternatives to minimize negative effects on their bowel functioning" (Tkachuk et al., 2003, p. 61). This CBGT was successful in treating IBS and in improving quality of life, and it was cost-effective. The research team reported the following:

> Significantly more CBGT patients reported reduced GI symptoms and abdominal pain, as compared with SMTC [symptom monitoring telephone contact, the usual treatment] patients, on post-treatment global ratings. CBGT patients were also more improved than SMTC patients in psychological functioning and health-related quality of life, and maintained these improvements at the 3-month follow-up evaluation. CBGT patients further experienced significantly reduced abdominal pain based on daily diary scores at the 3-month follow-up evaluation.... Effective group treatment is advantageous because it is more efficient and can be conducted at less cost to the health care system than individual treatment.... Changes in health-related quality of life reported by CBGT patients reflect improvements in time able to work, amount accomplished, and fewer limitations in per-

forming work/activity. These self-reported changes in behavior could have important implications for long-term adjustment (coping) and reduced health care utilization....Taken together, these results indicate that CBGT patients continued to benefit from the treatment they received, even though it was no longer being directly provided. (Tkachuk et al., 2003, pp. 65–66)

Using drugs for behavioral problems such as IBS raises health care costs and increases profits for the drug companies. More effective behavioral treatments lower health care costs for the individual consumer and for society as a whole.

PMS—"PMDD"—Premenstrual Difficulties.

Some women have difficulty with menstruation. However, the menstrual cycle, including some premenstrual symptoms, is a normal part of a woman's life—not a disorder. The menstrual cycle is natural—nothing is "disordered." Indeed, as portrayed in Anita Diamant's novel, *The Red Tent* (1997), menstruation was at times celebrated:

A gift to women that is not known among men, and this is the secret of blood...to men this is flux and distemper, bother and pain. They imagine we suffer and consider themselves lucky. We do not disabuse them...women give thanks—for repose and restoration, for the knowledge that life comes from between our legs, and that life costs blood. (p. 158)

First described in 1931, Katherine Dalton coined "premenstrual syndrome" (PMS) in 1953 and subsequently promoted and researched PMS. The symptoms, some of which directly contradict each other, total over 150, and they are far from unique or indicative of any internal problem. Dalton acknowledges, "The symptoms are commonplace and also occur with great frequency in men, children, and postmenopausal women" (1987, p. 135). It is puzzling how commonplace symptoms that occur frequently in children and men constitute a "disorder" in women. The current edition of the DSM refers to PMS as "premenstrual dysphoric disorder" (PMDD) under "disorders needing further study." This inclusion allowed doctors to prescribe drugs for PMS. It was not long until Prozac was repackaged in pretty purplish pills and renamed "Sarafem" with free samples readily offered to women for commonplace symptoms (Flora & Sellers, 2003).

Although described in 1931, the first medical journal article on PMS did not appear until 1964, and the first psychology journal not until 1966. But research on PMS "erupted" in the 1970s, according to Carol Tavris, because "when women's participation in the labor force is seen as a threat instead of a necessity, menstruation becomes a liability" (1992, p. 141). During World War II, women were required to "man" the factories, which they did admirably. "Rosy the riveter" did not have to take 4 days off each month. The war ended, and stereotypical women went back to being homemakers. But with women's liberation in the 1960s, women began to enter the workforce and compete with men for the same jobs. Men could maintain their advantage in the workplace by claiming that women became irrational and overly emotional for most of a week every month. Surely a man, argued to be more emotionally and physically stable, would make a better employee and a better employer. But along the way PMS got "co-opted" by biomedical researchers, by "the big money, the big guns" (Tavris, 1992, p. 141) and women began to falsely accept PMS as a life-limiting condition as a consequence of this co-opting.

In the process of becoming a disorder, PMS became a behaviorally conditioned monthly event for some women. The research revels that PMS is a product of conditioning, reinforcement, and observational learning, not actual physical severity. William Whitehead and his team of the Division of Digestive Disorders at the University of North Carolina studied 382 women and found that not actual physical severity but "childhood reinforcement and modeling of menstrual illness behavior had a significant influence on the number of physician visits for menstrual symptoms" (Whitehead, Crowell, Heller, Robinson, Schuster, & Horn, 1994, p. 547). Likewise, Canadian researchers Melanie Thompson and Mary Glick found that "consistent with previous research, care-seekers reported more reinforcement for adolescent menstrual illness behaviors than non-care-seekers. Care-seekers also reported their symptoms as more serious and more difficult to ignore. The perceived seriousness and severity of symptoms were both correlated with reinforcement for adolescent menstrual symptoms" (Thompson & Glick, 2000, p. 137). PMS symptoms are reinforced when expressing symptoms allows one to miss school, work, or other obligations, and when the symptoms produce sympathy and supportive behavior from others.

In a demonstration of the effects of observational learning on PMS, Mexican researchers gave two groups of women a survey on menstruation difficulty. They then showed one group of women an educational video on the menstrual cycle. Another group was shown a video describing PMS and aversive consequences of PMS. All women were given the survey again after their next menstruation. Women who watched the PMS video reported more severe premenstrual symptoms but the women who watched the video on menstruation did not (Marvan & Escobedo, 1999). Watching a video about stress fractures could not increase bone fractures. That watching a video on PMS increases PMS, coupled with the other studies, shows that PMS is not a result of any internal dysfunction (even in cases where menstruation does produce physical discomfort) but is largely a function of reinforcement, modeling, and observation. PMS is not the result of an internal dysfunction. PMS is a social construction. "Many women have a misperception about the meaning of PMS," report researchers Maria Marvan and Sandra Cortes-Iniestra. "Consequently, they amplify their premenstrual changes in recall, reflecting women's cultural stereotypes rather than their actual experiences" (2001, p. 276).

Even so, women who do miss work and stay in bed with complaints of PMS are in distress and may seek treatment. When they do seek treatment they are likely to be given a prescription for an SSRI, "Sarafem," previously known as "Prozac." Low serotonin levels have nothing to do with PMS, but selling serotonin drugs has everything to do with making money. The patent on Prozac was expiring, so Eli Lilly needed new, patent-protected, uses for the drug. It tried to show that the drug was effective in treating PMDD (DSM's new name for PMS). It funded a study published in 1995 (Steiner, Steinberg, Stewart et al.1995), illustrating that the drug produced "moderate improvement" in 52% of sufferers. Of course, this means that the drug did not help 48% and, furthermore, that the efficacy decreased considerably after 4 months. In sum, the drug was virtually no better than a placebo. Yet this study was enough for the FDA. The color of the Prozac pill was changed, and on July 6, 2000, the "new" drug, Sarafem, was approved by the FDA for PMDD. As listed on the information insert for the drug, some of the side effects include "tiredness, upset stomach, nervousness, dizziness, and difficulty concentrating." These side effects are some of the "symptoms" of PMDD. Ironically, then, it is possible that based on a psychiatrist's typical symptom inventory checklist diagnosis, the side effects from taking the drug to treat PMDD could actually produce a diagnosis of PMDD! No treatment at all is better than the drug "treatment" for PMS.

Conversely, the behavioral approach to treating women who have premenstrual distress is highly effective, with beneficial side effects. The behavioral approach involves healthy lifestyle changes, including exercise, improved nutrition, and perhaps CBT. Exercise, especially aerobic exercise, is more effective than Prozac or Sarafem in improving the symptoms of PMS. Exercise is "protective" against both physical symptoms, such as water retention, and psychological symptoms, including dysphoric mood (depression) anxiety, pain, and functional impairment (Bibi, 1996; Stoddard, 1999). A team of Georgetown University researchers found that following a vegetarian diet resulted in decreased painful menstruation and decreased pain and water retention and other symptoms (Barnard, Sciolli, Hurlock, & Berton, 2000). The greater efficacy of improved nutrition and exercise in reducing PMS symptoms should be enough to favor the behavioral approach over drugs. When the many other benefits of a more healthy lifestyle are contrasted to the adverse side effects of the drugs given for PMS, the choice is clear. The behavioral approach is superior.

To address false attributions and myths about PMS, CBT may be used to educate women about menstruation and health to teach new behaviors and new skills. Such approaches are highly effective (Flora & Sellers, 2003), much more effective than drugs, as Diana Taylor of the University of California-San Francisco found:

> A 75–85 percent reduction in PMS severity in women [results from] using a combination of dietary, exercise, and behavioral, cognitive, and environmental stress management strategies (Goodale, Domar, & Benson, 1990; Kirby, 1994). When compared to antidepressant drug therapy, the PMS-SMP [symptom management program (CBT)] was more effective in reducing premenstrual symptom severity and distress than studies testing fluoxetine [Prozac and Sarafem], which demonstrated 40-50 percent improvement in PMS severity, but up to one third of women will discontinue medication use due to drug side effects such as nausea, disturbed sleep, fatigue, and dizziness. (Taylor, 1999, p. 508)

Yet to "treat" women complaining of PMS, drugs remain "the first-line treatment option" (Pearlstein & Steiner, 2000) by psychiatrists. Given the superiority of behavioral treatment for PMS, this priority of drug treatment is shameful, if not unethical.

Urinary Incontinence

In *Behavioral vs. Drug Treatment for Urge Urinary Incontinence in Older Women*, published in the *JAMA*, a team of American researchers conclusively demonstrated the superiority of the behavioral treatment approach for the problem of urinary incontinence, a problem claimed to affect 38% of older women and costing over $16 billion each year (Burgio, Locher, Gooden, Hardin, McDowall, Dombrnski, & Condib, 1998). The participants consisted of 197 women, ages 55 to 92, assigned to either a placebo, a drug (2.5 mg of oxybutynin chloride, 3 times daily), or behavioral treatment. In the behavioral training

> [patients] were taught skills and strategies for preventing incontinence and provided with instructions for home practice. In visit 1, anorectal biofeedback [amplified feedback of muscle contraction] was used to help patients identify pelvic muscles and teach them how to contract and relax these muscles selectively while keeping abdominal muscles relaxed. Visit 2 was devoted to teaching patients how to respond adaptively to the sensation of urgency ("urge strategies"). Instead of rushing to the toilet, which increases intra-abdominal pressure and exposure to visual cues that can trigger incontinence, subjects were encouraged to pause, sit down if possible, relax the entire body, and contract pelvic muscles repeatedly to diminish urgency, inhibit detrusor contraction and prevent urine loss.... In visit 3, pelvic muscle biofeedback was repeated for subjects who had not achieved at least 50% reduction in frequency of accidents as documented on bladder diary.... Visit 4 was used to review progress, "fine-tune' home practice, and encourage persistence. Home practice included 45 pelvic muscle exercises every day (15 exercises 3 times daily). (Burgio et al., 1998, pp. 1996–1997)

Only four office visits and home practice, where women learned to control the functioning of their bodies, produced larger reductions in incontinence than taking drugs 3 times a day, every day. Specifically, "Behavioral training, which resulted in a 80.7% improvement, was significantly more effective than drug treatment (mean, 68.5% improvement)" (Burgio et al., 1998, pp. 1996–1997). Furthermore, patients receiving behavioral treatment reported more satisfaction and comfort than did the drugged patients:

> On every parameter, the behavioral group reported the highest perceived improvement and satisfaction with treatment progress. Of particular interest are the findings that 96.5% of the behavior group reported being comfortable enough with the treatment to continue indefinitely.... [Of drugged patients], only 54.7% said they would continue indefinitely and 75.5% said they wished to receive another form of treatment. (Burgio et al., 1998, pp. 1996-1997)

Satisfaction may be higher in part because "behavioral intervention has the advantage that incontinence can be reduced without the aversive effects that are common with pharmacological intervention" (Burgio et al., 1998, p. 1999). The researchers' conclusions regarding behavioral treatment for incontinence specifically hold true for behavioral treatment generally:

> The role of behavioral treatment was addressed at the National Institutes of Health-sponsored Consensus Conference on Urinary Incontinence in Adults. The consensus panel recommended that the least invasive or dangerous procedures should be tried first, and that for many forms of incontinence, this criterion is met by behavioral treatments. Behavioral treatment has also been recommended as a first-line treatment in the Clinical Practice Guidelines for Urinary Incontinence.... The behavioral procedures described ... are practical and can be implemented effectively by non-physician providers in outpatient office settings. A behavioral intervention with these characteristics has the potential for widespread application. Currently, drug treatment is readily available and widely used. The results of this study indicated

that behavioral treatment should also be made more available and offered routinely as an option for first-line treatment for urge incontinence. (Burgio et al., 1998, p. 2000)

Chapter 10

Conclusion

The least invasive or dangerous procedures should *always* be tried first, regardless of the specific problem. For virtually every type of psychological or behavioral problem, and for many medical problems, *the least invasive and dangerous and most effective procedures are behavioral treatments.* As such, behavioral treatments should be the first-line treatment. Currently the less effective, more dangerous, and more invasive but more profitable drugs are the first-line treatment. As has been shown repeatedly throughout this book, most behaviorial procedures are practical, can be implemented effectively in outpatient office settings, and have the potential for widespread application. If patients' well-being rather than corporate profit margins was the primary concern of the U.S health care system, then behavioral treatment would be made more available and offered routinely as an option for first-line treatment.

The Deepening Delusion and the Pharmaceutical Marketing Machine

America's deepening delusion that mental disorders are so prevalent that almost everyone suffers from at least one disease or another, and that everyone should be on one type of drug or another, is in no small part due to the successful marketing and promotion of drug companies. Pharmaceutical companies operate in the United States just as other companies do; they operate as businesses, with the intention of maximizing their profits. They must answer to shareholders and Wall Street analysts just as surely as IBM, Intel, and Microsoft must answer. The livelihood and job security of their CEOs and other officials depend not on how helpful or healthful their products are but on the profit they make. The pharmaceutical companies operate on a business model, not on a health model.

Instead of developing medications for serious problems that may only affect a very small population, like other companies that sell product, the drug companies *must generate a demand* by as many people as possible for that product, then market to that *artificially generated demand*. When a company holds a patent for a useful product it can make a huge profit. When the patent expires (usually 7 years), profits plunge. But if a company can find a new use for the product then it can patent the product for the new use, ensuring continued profit. Finding new uses for old drugs is standard procedure for drug companies. In "Disorders Made to Order," investigative reporter Brendan Koerner (2002) exposed several of the procedures drug companies use to generate demand for their products:

> [Step 1] A corporate-sponsored "disease awareness" campaign focuses on a mild psychiatric condition with a large pool of potential suffers. [Step 2] Companies fund studies that prove the drug's efficacy in treating the affliction, a necessary step in obtaining FDA approval for a new use, or "indication." [Step 3] Prominent doctors are enlisted to publicly affirm the malady's ubiquity. [Step 4] Public-relations firms launch campaigns to promote the new disease, using dramatic statistics from corporate-sponsored studies. [Step 5] Finally, patient groups are recruited to serve as the "public face" of the condition, supply quotes and compelling human stories for the media; many of the groups are heavily subsidized by drug makers, and some operate directly out of the offices of drug companies' PR firms. (Koerner, 2002, p. 60)

Following these steps, the drug companies positioned the SSRIs, Prozac, Paxil, and Zoloft into money-making machines. When supplying SSRIs for depression played out, patents expired, and profits thinned, a new market was need. Backed by company-funded studies, or in-house studies, the companies sought FDA approval for "new indications" (using the drugs to treat problems for which they were not originally approved). The "disorders" generalized anxiety, social anxiety, and, more recently, premenstrual dysphoric disorder (e.g., "PMS") (see previous chapter) were targeted. Because these disorders *were* "extremely rare," PR companies were launched, convincing millions of Americans with normal feelings and emotions that they actually suffered from disorders for having these feelings. Gullibility to slick advertising and PR schemes is all most of these victims are suffering from.

Indeed, as detailed by Allen Horwitz, professor at Rutgers University Institute of Health, Health Care Policy, and Aging, researching this formula to "create an illness where none exists to promote drugs sales" is *exactly* what occurred with sexual dysfunction and Viagra. First the study "Sexual Dysfunction in the United States" was published in the highly prestigious *Journal of the American Medical Association (JAMA)* (Laumann, Paik, & Rosen, 1999), which reported that 43% of women and 31% of men suffered from sexual dysfunction during the preceding year. A national epidemic of mental illness! But, as Horwitz notes,

These huge numbers result from a failure to use a valid definition of mental disorder that distinguishes internal dysfunctions from expectable results of social stressors or of diminished, but normal, interest in having sex. Symptoms such as the failure to obtain an erection...can stem from well-adjusted couples who no longer have a strong interest in sexual relationships. They might also stem from boring or inept sexual partners or from unsatisfactory or abusive relationships. Indeed, this study finds that the best predictor of "sexual dysfunction" is low satisfaction with one's partner.... The assumption that the presence of symptoms, regardless of what factors account for them, represents and individual dysfunction is unwarranted.... [Yet] the authors of the *JAMA* study conclude that sexual dysfunction is a "public health" problem that calls for increased provision of medical therapies, especially medications.... The authors of this study assume that people with bad or boring interpersonal relationships should remedy their condition by taking drugs that increase their sexual stimulation. (Horwitz, 2002, pp. 92–93)

Why would supposedly reputable researchers and a top-rated medical journal push the idea of an epidemic of sexual dysfunction? According to Horwitz:

> the study was done shortly after a new drug, Viagra, came on the market, with sales that exceeded $1 billion the first year.... Calling people with problems in their interpersonal relationships "sexually dysfunctional" may help the business of the pharmaceutical company that sponsored the research, but it fundamentally mischaracterizes most of the problems the study uncovers. (Horwitz, 2002, p. 94)

Horwitz has found that this procedure of creating an illness epidemic when no internal dysfunctions exist in order to promote drug sales also has occurred with several other "disorders," leading him to conclude that "many of the fifty million Americans who meet the criteria for a mental disorder in community studies do not have valid disorders but suffer from distress that is rooted in stressful social arrangements that will disappear when these situations improve" (Horwitz, 2002, p. 222). Furthermore, when troubled relationships or actual dysfunction, sexual or otherwise, do exist, they are treated more effectively and with behavioral treatments than with drug treatments. The behavioral treatments have beneficial side effects, such as improved social skills, better functioning, and empowerment, while the drug approaches have adverse side effects.

"Generalized anxiety disorder" and "social phobia" are additional cases in point. According to the American Psychiatric Association's *Diagnostic and Statistical Manual* (mental health's diagnostic bible, published by a drug-friendly organization), only 2% of the population will "experience enough impairment or distress to warrant a diagnosis of social phobia." But to boost sales of their SSRI, SmithKline's PR firm promoted the disorder, claiming that social phobia "affects up to 13.3% of the population" and is "the third most common psychiatric disorder in the United States, after depression and alcoholism" (Koerner, 2002, p. 61). As a result of this PR campaign, hundreds of stories on social phobia appeared in the U.S. media, and sales of Paxil soared, as did company profits.

Another consequence of this campaign was that millions of people were medicated with drugs that the FDA now requires their makers to state (e.g., admit in writing) that suicidal thoughts by adolescents is a side effect of the drugs. Possible suicides are not an acceptable trade-off for taking drugs in an attempt to reduce the anxiety that a teenager may have over the prom or a college entrance examination. No one, other than shareholders, profits from the PR campaign to promote SSRI drugs for social anxiety or generalized anxiety.

Unfortunately, the "invent an epidemic when none exists" tactic to push drugs is not limited to SSRI sales, but it is used for any product when there is a possibility of profit, including many unnecessary drugs. One consequence is that children are unnecessarily put on ADHD medications. The ADD and ADHD drugs are promoted by false claims, that the flawed—drug-funded—MTA and other studies "proved" that drugs are the most effective "treatment" (see the chapter on ADHD). The full-page advertisement pushing the amphetamine Adderall regularly appears in the *Parade* magazine that accompanies many Sunday papers across the country. "Increase math scores one letter grade" is the claim. Nowhere in the ad is "Do your homework," "Practice," "Study," "Get enough sleep," "Hire a tutor," or "Parental involvement" even hinted at. "Drug your children for happier days" is the clear message.

THE EPIDEMIC OF "MENTAL ILLNESS EPIDEMICS"

People do not have more personal, social, sexual, or psychological problems than they had in the past. They were simply and correctly recognized as problems, some admittedly very difficult problems, but problems nevertheless. They were not, as they are now, incorrectly considered "disorders." This increase in calling problems "disorders" is not merely the view of a critic, but a reality. As Carol Tavris has noted:

> The Diagnostic and Statistical Manual of Mental Disorders, the bible of psychiatry, contains a list of mental disorders that are compensable by insurance companies. As the territory of psychiatry and clinical psychology has expanded, so has the number of treatable problems. In 1968, the manual contained 66 disorders; in the 1987 edition, it had 261 disorders... and by the fourth edition in 1994, it had nearly 400 disorders. The DSM includes not only serious disorders such as schizophrenia and other psychoses, but also normal problems for which people seek help, including tobacco dependence, reading problems, and sexual complaints.... [Furthermore] most definitions of mental disorder are a matter of subjective clinical consensus, not science. (2001, p. 102)

As outlined by Allan Horwitz (2002), this increase in disorders was not happenstance but was, and is, an ongoing product of deliberate social construction. First, psychiatry has always struggled to be respected as a legitimate branch of medicine (see Gelman, 1999, for collaboration). With Freud, "dynamic psychiatry" emerged, giving psychiatry a brief period of respectability. However, two primary factors limited dynamic psychiatry's ability to empower psychiatry as a respected branch of medicine. First, it was simply unscientific: "An apocryphal statement is apt in this regard: 'Psychotherapy is an undefined technique applied to unspecified problems with unpredictable outcome. For this technique we recommend rigorous training' (quoted in Grob, 1991, 127)" (Horwitz, 2002, p. 60). Second, to the very limited extent that psychoanalysis might be helpful, humanistic psychology, or any other of dozens of new age psychobabble therapies, proved to be equally as effective or equally as ineffective—whichever the case may be.

Therefore, in a deliberate attempt to gain respectability, psychiatry turned from dynamic psychiatry to a medical diagnostic model of practice. "The publication of the *Diagnostic and Statistical Manual* (DSM-III) in 1980 marked a second revolution in thinking about mental illness. The promulgators of the DSM-III overthrew the broad, continuous, and vague concepts of dynamic psychiatry and reclaimed the categorical illnesses of asylum psychiatry" (Horwitz, 2002, p. 2). But because during the Freudian dynamic era of psychiatry, psychiatrists had begun to see everyday people with everyday problems, and they did not want to lose this client base, this revenue stream, psychiatry began to categorize everyday problems as "disorders." And since a "disorder" implies an *internal dysfunction*, it was a minor and natural step for the pharmaceutical companies to be in cahoots with psychiatry. Together, the psychiatric profession and the pharmaceutical companies have worked to develop an ever-increasing number of "disorders" to be treated with profitable drugs targeted at the supposed internal dysfunction that was supposedly behind the alleged disorder.

> The use of various psychopharmacological agents now dominates the psychiatric profession. Treatments for mental illness are no longer directed at a small number of seriously ill persons. Instead, they are aimed at the many millions of people who presumably have some mental disorder.... Pervasive educational and advertising campaigns urge those sufferers who are not yet in treatment to recognize that they have genuine disorders that should be relieved through medication. (Horwitz, 2002, p. 4)

Horwitz carefully develops the case that most of these so-called disorders are not caused by internal dysfunction, but that most "mental illness" is a normal response to a stressful, dysfunctional life situation. For example:

> People who become depressed and anxious or who develop psychophysiological symptoms when they struggle with stressful life events, difficulties in interpersonal relationships, uncertain futures, bad jobs, and limited resources, react in [an] *appropriate* way to their environments; they do not have internal dysfunctions and so are not mentally disordered if their symptoms disappear when their social circumstances change....Distress that emerges from social conditions is neither a mental disorder nor a distinct disease condition. (Horwitz, 2002, p. 14, italics in original)

Claims from psychiatrists and the pharmaceutical companies notwithstanding, taking drugs cannot change such circumstances. But behavior therapy, behavioral training, empowers people to ameliorate or remedy stressful life events. Behavioral therapy teaches interpersonal skills to improve interpersonal relationships. Behavioral approaches most effectively teach vocational skills to improve job prospects and future possibilities. Behavioral therapies foster optimism. In comparison, drug therapy is likely to foster hopelessness regarding one's current situation and future prospects.

UNQUESTIONED ACCEPTANCE

Although most problems listed as disorders in the DSM are a product of "subjective clinical consensus, not science" (Tavris, 2001, p. 102), "psychiatrists, epidemiologists, and clinicians simply accept as mental disorders whatever conditions the DSM lists...without questioning whether the conditions they measure are valid disorders or not" (Horwitz, 2002, pp. 18–19). Family doctors, pediatricians, and mental health workers of all stripes also uncritically accept the DSM as factual, even though it is far from it.

Unfortunately this uncritical acceptance of the DSM may be an unavoidable by-product of the U.S. educational system. Beginning in middle school, future medical doctors and many future PhDs must learn

vast amounts of biology, chemistry, mathematics, and other often difficult topics that require much memorization. The students are reinforced
with passing grades for memorizing the material. They are not reinforced
for asking their instructors if the material being presented is valid or not.
For most, this high-pressure memorization mode continues through
graduate school and medical school. Thus when students are given a list
of supposed "disorders" and a checklist of "symptoms," they memorize
them. The students are unlikely to ask whether or not the entire enter-
prise is a valid one. The students memorize, graduate, and get their
degrees, and as a consequence, they are recognized as "experts" by society
at large. These "experts" of "psychological disorders" then "educate" less-
educated teachers, caseworkers, and other bachelors' or masters' level
professionals. These less-educated people are the ones who are then considered the "experts" by naive or uneducated people who are dealing with
behavioral difficulties firsthand. These "experts" are in direct contact
with the troubled people and often first suggest that someone may have
a "disorder" that supposedly is best treated with drugs.

The person who has a behavioral difficulty, the parent, or spouse is
also likely to uncritically accept this suggestion as fact. A parent is likely
to ask, "They are the experts, so who am I to question?" This uncritical
acceptance is a product of the U.S. medical care system. Following doctors' directions is reinforced. When a doctor tells parents that their child
has measles and to give the child a drug to cure it, the child gets better if
the directions are followed. When a doctor tells parents that their child
has an infection and to give the child a drug to cure it, the child gets
better if the directions are followed. As a result of this reinforcement history, when a doctor tells parents that their child has a "psychological disorder" (ADHD, depression, GAD) and to give the child a drug to cure
it, the parents will likely follow those directions and give the child the
drug. Unfortunately, because the majority of behavioral difficulties are a
product of problematic behavior-environment interactions and not
internal dysfunctions, in this case following an "expert's" directions will
not help.

COMPROMISED SCIENCE, COMPROMISED ETHICS

Just as court juries are supposed to objectively analyze the evidence to
reach unbiased conclusions, researchers are supposed to objectively analyze results to reach unbiased conclusions. But allowing the drug compa-

nies to fund studies that "prove" the drug's efficacy is equivalent to allow-ing lawyers to pay juries to "prove" their client's case. It is simply dishon-est and unethical, but this is exactly what happens. The pharmaceutical "industry sponsors provide approximately 70 percent of the funding for clinical drug trials in the United States" (Mello, Clarridge, & Studdert, 2005, p. 2202). Since they control the purse strings, they try to control the results, putting ethics and science into question. Harvard researchers Michelle Mello, PhD, and her colleagues surveyed 107 medical centers that reported that many sponsors tried to *control* statistical analysis, *control* reporting, and *control* sharing of data that the public is led to believe is independent and objective. In effect, the drug companies are saying, "We paid for this study, so now you find and report what we want you to report." According to Mello:

> Our findings lend empirical support to concern expressed in previous commentary about the threat to academic freedom that restrictive contractual provisions may present. They extend previous study findings that a substantial proportion of industry-academic research centers across a wide range of fields (including medicine) *permitted sponsors to delete informa-tion from publications and delay publications....* Industry spon-sors could "form shop," channeling their studies to relatively permissive institutions... [Many disputes between sponsors and institutions] had embedded ethical issues. For example, in one case, the sponsor refused to send the final payment because it did not approve the research report, "apparently because they didn't like the results of the study." (Mello et al., 2005, pp. 2208–2209, italics added)

Thus in many cases research that was supposed to independently determine whether a treatment is effective may have been strongly influ-enced or controlled by the drug company that stands to make billions of dollars in profits if the drug is reported to be effective and free of adverse side effects. This pharmaceutical influence and pressure continue at the Food and Drug Administration (FDA)—an agency that is supposed to protect consumers. In fact, it is not a stretch to argue that the FDA is not controlled by the government, not controlled by the taxpayers, and not controlled by the citizens of the United States and our elected repre-sentatives. No, the FDA is controlled by those that support and main-tain it with their money—the drug companies. The drug companies lobbying pressure was rewarded, with Congress basically ceding control of the FDA to the companies it was meant to control. As noted by Carl Elliott of the Center for Bioethics at the University of Minnesota:

> The drug industry increased pressure on the FDA to let companies bring drugs to the market more quickly. As a result, in 1992 Congress passed the Prescription Drug User Fee Act, under which drug companies pay a variety of fees to the FDA, with the aim of speeding up drug approval (thereby making the drug industry a major funder of the agency set up to regulate it). In 1997 the FDA dropped most restrictions on direct-to-consumer advertising of prescription drugs, opening the gate for the eventual Levitra ads on Super Bowl Sunday and Zoloft cartoons during daytime television shows. (Elliott, 2006, p. 88)

A similar relationship would be to have would-be immigrants to the United States pay to fund the U.S. border patrol. Citizens could not expect a well-protected border under such an arrangement. But that is the arrangement between the FDA and the drug companies, and as a consequence citizens are not well protected by the FDA. The critical difference in this analogy is that most immigrants do not have the money to pay for the border patrol, but the drug companies do have the money to pay the FDA. In fact, in addition to the FDA, the pressure and influence peddling from drug companies is a full-court press targeting medical residents, doctors, and consumers, all in the name of profit—not in the name of helping people.

As a case in point, direct-to-consumer advertising is enormously effective. For every dollar spent on direct-to-consumer advertising, there is a $4 return. Not surprisingly, Harvard researchers Meredith Rosenthal and her team found that between 1996 and 2000, funding for direct-to-consumer advertising grew "disproportionately" to other forms of promotion, from $791 million to over $2.5 billion, a threefold increase in only 4 years (Rosenthal, Berndt, Donohue, Frank, & Epstein, 2002). The number increased to $3.2 billion in 2003. Of course, the drug companies claim that such advertisements are for public information only—they are "educational." The truth is that such tactics do not educate, but they do swell profits.

Consider a woman whose relationship with her husband is in a rough patch. Her company is downsizing, so she is laid off after 15 years, and her daughter may flunk out of high school. To top it all off, it has been rainy and cold for the past 3 weeks! It would be completely normal to feel sad and depressed during such a time. But hallelujah! She sees an advertisement on TV suggesting that her sadness may be due to a chemical imbalance, and that she should ask her doctor about treating it with drugs. So she does and is put on an SSRI. She may feel better, but she will still have difficulties with her husband, she will still be out of work, and her daughter will still have trouble at school if she has not already dropped out. These direct-to-consumer advertising campaigns do not tell the unhappy person that behavioral couples therapy may open the line of communication with her husband and help reestablish a mutually reinforcing relationship. The advertisements do not educate the woman about possible vocational training or provide her with job interview skills, as can behavioral therapy (but on her job applications, she may have to indicate that she is now on drugs for a "mental problem"). The advertisements do not give her information about behavioral parent training or about tutoring skills to help her daughter. No, they get her on drugs. Direct-to-consumer advertisements are not educational, they are anti-educational.

Direct-to-consumer advertising works because consumers use it to diagnose themselves and their families. They then suggest their ill-informed diagnoses to their doctors and which drugs they want for it. Doctors usually comply. In a study published in the *Journal of the American Medical Association*, a team of researchers, led by Richard Kravitz, University of California, Davis, sent patients to doctors in three U.S. cities (Kravitz, Epslein, Feldman, et al., 2005). Patients, in over 298 unannounced visits, complained of either major depression or an adjustment disorder and either requested nothing, general medication, or a brand-specific drug. When patients complained of depression and made no request, they were given a prescription 31% of the time. But when they complained of depression and made a specific request—for Paxil— they were given a prescription 51% of the time. When patients complained of adjustment difficulties and made no request, they were given a prescription just 10% of the time. But shockingly, *when patients complained of adjustment difficulty and made a specific request, they were given a prescription for antidepressant drugs 55% of the time.* That is worth repeating: Based on just a single doctor visit, simply complaining of adjustment difficulty and suggesting a drug resulted in patients receiving a prescription for a powerful drug over half the time.

Many doctors claim that they are not influenced by such requests or by gifts from pharmaceutical sales reps. But they are wrong. The more doctors are wined, dined, and even bribed the more likely they are to prescribe a sales rep's company's drugs (Elliott, 2006). That is why sales reps can get rich and why the number of sales reps doubled from 1996 to 2001, to 90,000 reps. The influence is so pervasive that "in 2001 the AMA launched a campaign to educate doctors about the ethical perils of pharmaceutical gifts [but the campaign was laughable because] it undercut its message by funding the campaign with money from the pharmaceutical industry" (Elliott, 2006, pp. 89–90). Furthermore, "pharmaceutical companies were providing 90 percent of the $1 billion spent annually on continuing medical education events, which doctors must attend in order to maintain their licensure" (Elliott, 2006, p. 91). Therefore, often when doctors should be learning about the latest innovations in care they are instead being wined and dined while listening to what amounts to little more than a slick sales pitch. Unfortunately, dangerous and often unnecessary drugs are being pitched.

These dangerous and unnecessary drugs not only include antidepressants for people who have adjustment problems—people who could be better helped by learning new behavioral skills, or by being taught how to make actual behavioral adjustments. Dangerous and unnecessary amphetamine drugs also are increasingly being given to children and adults as a result of direct-to-consumer advertising and sales pitches to doctors. Between 2000 and 2004, the number of adults labeled "ADHD" and put on amphetamines or other powerful stimulants doubled, largely because of direct-to-consumer advertising and a lax FDA. "The surge in adult use came amid the growing direct-to-consumer advertising and the Food and Drug Administration's approval for the first time of drugs to treat adult ADHD" (Elias, 2005, p. 1). Similar increases occurred for children, for example, 56 of 1,000 (5.6%) of boys ages 10 to 19 were on such drugs in 2000; by 2004, the number had swelled to 80 per 1,000; 8% of all U.S. boys ages 10–19 are being drugged (Elias, 2006)! This increase does not reflect an epidemic of any disorder or improved treatment of any disorder. The United States consumes over 4 times as much stimulant drug medication as the rest of the world combined, not because people in the U.S. are 4 times as hyperactive and deficit in attention as the rest of the world. No, the increasing rate of consumption is a case of business marketing success, plain and simple. But this business success comes at a price to those who are sold the bill of goods.

Heart attacks, strokes, hallucinations, and death are all possible side effects of taking stimulant ADHD drugs. On February 9, 2006, the

FDA's Drug Safety and Risk Management advisory committee voted to but a "black box" warning on all ADHD drugs, including Adderall, Concerta, Focalin, Metadate, Methylin, and Ritalin. The warning was that taking the drugs may result in *sudden death, heart attacks,* or *strokes.* The committee advised using this black box warning because at least 25 children and adults died between 1999 and 2003 as a result of taking these drugs. It is very possible that these stimulant drugs cause or compound cardiovascular problems. No one should be surprised that taking powerful amphetamines or other chemical stimulants day after day, year after year, can result in serious health problems, even death. But it should be surprising, and an outrage, that over 31 million Americans are in fact being prescribed such drugs. "It's being handed out like candy," according to Jacqueline Bessner, whose 15-year-old daughter, Leanne, hanged herself after being put on Concerta (Bridges, 2006, p. 2). The unnecessary drugging of children is especially outrageous when effective, nondrug behavioral training methods are available to improve children's attention and overactivity problems.

Unfortunately, yielding to lobbying efforts, on March 22, 2006, another FDA committee, the Pediatric Advisory Committee, backed off from recommending the strong black box warning. Instead it recommended a watered down guide that would include the warning along with other information. "The FDA was poised Wednesday to follow the more recent [lax] recommendations" (Bridges, 2006, p. 1).

Despite this minor victory for the pharmaceutical companies, the dangers of these drugs are increasingly coming to the forefront. The same week the Pediatric Advisory Committee backed off from the black box warning, that ADHD posed cardiovascular dangers, the committee said ADHD medications for children needed to carry a warning about hallucinations! " 'We see case upon case of these children who do experience these hallucinations,' Rosemary Johann-Laing of the FDA's office of Drug Safety told the committee" (Rubin, 2006, p. 1). It should not be surprising that these drugs produce hallucinations. Their chemical cousins, the illegal street drugs—methamphetamine, "ecstacy," and the like—are often taken specifically for their ability to produce hallucinatory effects. While not surprising, it is disheartening that millions upon millions of American children are given these drugs by misinformed parents, doctors, and school nurses.

The drug companies are not only successful in getting the nation's children (and increasing numbers of adults) on ADHD drugs but on antidepressant drugs as well. This success has not come without grave problems, such as suicide. As a result of children and adolescents who committed suicide while on SSRI drugs in 2004, the FDA's Pediatric Advisory Committee did vote to put suicide black box warnings on SSRI drugs.

As if powerful stimulants and SSRIs were not enough, as a team of Vanderbilt University Medical researchers just reported, there is an alarming growth in prescribing antipsychotic drugs to children. In just 7 years there has been a *fivefold increase* in prescriptions for neuropeltics— the major tranquilizers (thioridazine hydrochloride, haloperidol, promazine, clozapine, and others)—for American children. Furthermore, many of those prescribing have no specific training regarding their use, except perhaps a drug rep's sales pitch. Even more alarming, there has been no increase in childhood rates of schizophrenia, therefore, these children are being given these very powerful, happiness reducing drugs in a vain attempt to deal with perceived behavioral difficulties.

> Between 1995 and 2002, the outpatient prescribing of antipsychotics for children in the United States increased nearly fivefold. More than 30% of the prescriptions were from nonmental health providers. In addition, more than half of the antipsychotic prescriptions were for behavioral indications or affective disorders, conditions for which antipsychotics have not been carefully studied in children. It does not appear that temporal increases in serious mental health disorders such as schizophrenia accounted for the increases seen in this study, as recent studies do not suggest significant increases in the incidence in schizophrenia.... The increased prescribing of antipsychotic medications in children for behavioral indications is disconcerting given the paucity of information on the overall benefits and risks of this class of medications in children.... Over 50% of the antipsychotic prescriptions were for a diagnosis for which antipsychotics have not been studied in children. There may be little recognized benefits to these medications in many of the children receiving them, and potential risks do exist. (Cooper, Arbogast, Ding, Hickson, Fuchs, & Roy, 2006, pp. 81–82)

Why risk heart attacks, strokes, hallucinations, and death when behavioral treatments are more effective and empowering and have only beneficial side effects? Despite the superiority of behavioral treatment, the pharmaceutical money machine continues to roll, with harmful consequences in its wake. The problems with attempting to medicate behavioral difficulties continue to surface: "June 30, 2005—FDA officials are considering altering the drug's [Concerta] label to more clearly alert doctors as well as parents of children with ADHD about potential medication-related side effects, including visual hallucination, psychotic episodes, and aggressive or violent behavior" (Zwillich, 2005b). "July 1, 2005—The FDA has issued a public health advisory regarding data linking the possibility of an increased risk of suicidal behavior in adults taking antidepressants" (Smith, 2005). Even though much more effective and less expensive behavioral treatments exist, the drug companies not only use the media to manufacture the perceived need for these dangerous drugs, with hundreds of millions spent on advertising, they also spare no expense in manipulating lawmakers to pass drug-friendly laws. According to the Center for Public Integrity, drug companies spent more than any other business sector, a record $128 million in 2004, lobbying U.S. politicians.

The result of this campaign is an epidemic of prescription drug use and abuse for many problems that are most effectively addressed without using drugs at all. A comprehensive 3-year study of prescription opioids (e.g., Oxycontin, Vicodin), central nervous system (CNS) depressants (e.g., Valium, Xanax), and CNS stimulants (e.g., Ritalin, Adderall), utilizing 15 national data sets, interviews, focus groups, and surveys of 979 physicians and 1,030 pharmacists by the National Center on Addiction and Substance Abuse at Columbia University (CASA), "found that from 1992 to 2003, while the U.S. population increased 14 percent, the number of 12- to 17-year-olds who abused controlled prescription drugs jumped 212 percent, and the number of adults 18 and older abusing drugs climbed 81 percent" (CASA, 2005). While this soaring drug use provides profits for the drug companies, society suffers. These supposedly helpful drugs, many of which have been discredited and shown to be ineffective in hundreds of studies (many of which are described in this book), are causing more problems than they solve. According to Joseph Califano, CASA chairman and former U.S. Secretary of Health Education and Welfare, "Our nation is in the throes of an epidemic of controlled prescription drug abuse and addiction" (CASA, 2005). This epidemic is not without consequences. Addiction, suicide, and crime are some of the consequences. These doctor-prescribed drugs are often the "gateway" to more dangerous illegal drugs such as heroin and methamphetamine.

The source for these deadly legal drugs is not the street corner pusher but the family's medicine cabinet. The medicine cabinet is now filled with legally obtained drugs from pharmacists who filled doctors' legal prescriptions. In many cases, the doctors have provided these prescriptions because they have been "educated" about their supposed effectiveness by pharmaceutical representatives and by pharmaceutical-company-sponsored "continuing education" seminars. The resolution of the epidemic, should there be one, will come only when health and mental health professionals become widely educated about and trained to apply safe and more effective behavioral treatments for behavioral, psychological and health problems. Eventually the United States will have to decide whether it wants a system where the health, well-being, and happiness of its citizensare primary, or whether, as is the current case, the behavioral problems of the people provide just another source of income for the privileged to exploit.

A behavioral balance is possible. America's drug dependency is curable. But the cure is not more and better drugs. The cure includes ameliorating stressful living conditions that give rise to behavioral, adjustment, and mood difficulties in the first place. When it is not possible to ameliorate such conditions, the cure involves teaching people behavioral skills in order to cope and adjust to their less-than-ideal living situation. With children, the cure involves providing more nurturing, reinforcing home and school environments; it involves making behavioral parent training more available and, when conditions warrant, using effective procedures such as home point systems and daily report cards. The cure comes in teaching people who have anxiety problems the skills necessary to confront their problems and difficulties in order to live fuller lives. Every life has limitations and shortcomings. Therefore, rather than obsessing about one's limitations, whitewashing limitations with drugs, or using limitations as an excuse, when necessary the cure involves teaching one to accept or overcome one's limitations and commiting to living a more valued, reinforcing life.

References

American Psychiatric Association. (1994). *Diagnostic and statistical manual of mental disorders* (4th ed.). Washington, DC: Author.

Anderson, D. A., & Maloney, K. C. (2001). Efficacy of cognitive-behavioral therapy on the core symptoms of bulimia nervosa. *Clinical Psychology Review, 21,* 971–988.

Angell, M., Utiger, R, D., & Wood, A. J. J. (2000). Disclosure of authors' conflicts of interest: A follow-up. *New England Journal of Medicine, 342,* 1901–1902.

Antonuccio, D. (1995). Psychotherapy for depression: No stronger medicine. *American Psychologist, 50,* 450–452.

Antony, M. M., & Swinson, R. P. (2001). Comparative and combined treatments for obsessive-compulsive disorder. In M. T. Sammons & N. B. Schmidt (Eds.), *Combined treatments for mental disorders* (pp. 53–80) Washington DC: American Psychological Association.

Argyle, M. (1986). Social skills and the analysis of situations and conversations. In C. R. Hollin & P. Trower (Eds.), *Handbook of social skills training* (Vol. 2) (pp. 185–216). New York: Pergamon.

Arnold, L. E., Chuang, S., Davies, M., Abikoff, H. B., et al. (2004). Nine months of multicomponent behavioral treatment for ADHD and effectiveness of MTA fading procedures. *Journal of Abnormal Child Psychology, 32,* 39–51.

Arntz, A. (2003). Cognitive therapy versus applied relaxation as treatment of generalized anxiety disorder. *Behavior Research and Therapy, 41,* 633–646.

Attia, E., Haiman, C., Walsh, B. T., & Flater, S. R. (1998). Does fluoxetine augment the inpatient treatment of anorexia nervosa? *American Journal of Psychiatry, 155,* 548–551.

Ayllon, T., Layman, D., & Kandel, H. J. (1975). A behavioral-educational alternative to drug control of hyperactive children. *Journal of Applied Behavior Analysis, 8,* 137–146.

Azar, B. (1995, November). Social-phobia treatments may also work for problem shyness. *APA Monitor,* 24.

Babyak, M., Blumenthal, J. A., Herman, S., Khatri, P., Doraiswamy, M., Moore, K., Craighead, W. E., Baldewicz, T. T., & Krishnan, K. R. (2000). Exercise treatment for major depression: Maintenance of therapeutic benefit at 10 months. *Psychosomatic Medicine, 62*(5), 633–638.

Bach, P., & Hayes, S. C. (2002). The use of acceptance and commitment therapy to prevent the rehospitalization of psychotic patients: A randomized controlled trial. *Journal of Consulting and Clinical Psychology, 70,* 1129–1139.

Ballenger, J. C. (1999). Current treatments of the anxiety disorders in adults. *Biological Psychiatry, 46,* 1579–1594.

Barlow, D. H., & Durand, V. M. (1999). *Abnormal Psychology, 2nd ed.* Pacific Grove, CA: Brooks/Cole.

Barlow, D. H., & Durand, V. M. (2005). *Abnormal Psychology, 4th ed.* Pacific Grove, CA: Brooks/Cole.

Barlow, D. H., Raffa, S. D., & Cohen, E. M. (2002). Psychosocial treatments for panic disorders, phobias, and generalized anxiety disorder. In P. E. Nathan & J. M. Gorman (Eds.), *A guide to treatments that work,* (pp. 301–336). New York: Oxford University Press.

Barnard, N. D., Scialli, A. R., Hurlock, D., & Berton, P. (2000). Diet and sex-hormone binding globulin, dysmenorrhea, and premenstrual symptoms. *Obstetrics and Gynecology, 95,* 245–250.

Beck, A. (1976). Cognitive *Therapy and the emotional disorders.* New York: International University Press.

Begley, S., & Biddle, N. A. (1996, February 26). For the obsessed, the mind can fix the brain. *Newsweek,* 60.

Bibi, K. W. (1996). The effects of aerobic exercise on premenstrual syndrome symptoms. *Dissertation Abstracts International: Section B: The Sciences and Engineering, 56,* 6678.

Blanchard, E. B., & Malamood, H. S. (1996). Psychological treatment of irritable bowel syndrome. *Professional Psychology: Research and Practice, 27,* 241–244.

Bond, A. J., Wingrove, J., Curran, H. V., & Lader, M. H. (2002). Treatment of generalised anxiety disorder with a short course of psychological therapy, combined with buspirone or placebo. *Journal of Affective Disorders, 72,* 267–271.

Bonne, J. (2003). "Go pills": A war on drugs? *Retrieved 11/30/2004 from http://www.msnbc.msn.com/id/307189.*

Borkovec, T. D., & Costello, E. (1993). Efficacy of applied relaxation and cognitive-behavioral therapy in the treatment of generalized anxiety disorder. *Journal of Consulting and Clinical Psychology, 61,* 611–619.

Bosworth, H. B., Hays, J. C., George, L. K., & Steffens, D. C. (2002). Psychosocial and clinical predictors of unipolar depression outcome in older adults. *International Journal of Geriatric Psychiatry, 17,* 238–246.

Bower, B. (1991). Pumped up and strung out. *Science News, 140,* 30–31.

Brenner, H. D., Hodel, B., Roder, V., & Corrigan, P. (1992). Treatment of cognitive dysfunction and behavioral deficits in schizophrenia. *Schizophrenia Bulletin, 18,* 21–26.

Bridges, A. (2006, March 22). Advisers reject strong ADHD warnings. Retrieved 3/27/2004 from *http://www.washingtonpost.com/wp-dyn/content/article/2006/02/22/ AR2006032200284.*

Brigham, T. A., Graubard, P. S., & Stans, A. (1972). An analysis of effects of sequential reinforcement contingencies on aspects of composition. *Journal of Applied Behavior Analysis, 5,* 421–429.

Brink, S. (2000, March 6). Tools to treat a troubled child. *U.S. News and World Report,* 49.

Brody, A. L., Saxena, S., Schwartz, J. M., Stoessel, P. W., Maidment, K., Phelps, M. E., & Baxter. L. R. (1998). FDG-PET predictors of response to behavioral therapy and pharmacotherapy in obsessive-compulsive disorder. *Psychiatry Research: Neuroimaging, 84,* 1–6.

Burgio, K. L., Locher, J. L., Goode, P. S., Hardin, J. M., McDowell, B. J., Dombrowski, M., & Candib, D. (1998). Behavioral vs. drug treatment for urge urinary incontinence in older women. *Journal of the American Medical Association, 280,* 1995–2000.

Calsyn, R. J., & Winter, J. P. (2002). Social support, psychiatric symptoms, and housing: A causal analysis. *Journal of Community Psychology, 30,* 247–259.

Cameron, J., Banko, K. M., & Pierce, W. D. (2001). Pervasive negative effects of rewards on intrinsic motivation: The myth continues. *Behavior Analyst, 24,* 1–44.

Carlat, D. J., Camargo, C. A., Jr., & Herzog, D. B. (1997). Eating disorders in males: A report on 135 patients. *American Journal of Psychiatry, 154,* 1127–1132.

Carter, F. A., McIntosh, V. V. W., Joyce, P. R., Sullivan, P. F., & Bulik, C. M. (2003). Role of exposure with response prevention in cognitive-behavioral therapy for bulimia nervosa: Three-year follow-up results. *International Journal of Eating Disorders, XX,* 127–135.

CASA. (2005, July 7). *More than 15 million Americans abuse opioids, depressants, stimulants; Teen abuse triples in 10 years.* New York: CASA at Columbia University.

CBC News Online (2004). *Go-pills, bombs, & friendly fire.* Retrieved 11/19/2006 from *http://www.cbc.ca/news/background/friendlyfire/ gopills.html.*

Clark, D. B., & Stewart, A. W. (1991). The assessment and treatment of performance anxiety in musicians. *American Journal of Psychiatry, 148,* 598–605.

Cleghorn, J. M., Franco, S., Szechtman, B., Kaplan, R. D., Szechtman, H., Brown, G. M., Nahmias, C., & Garnett, E. S. (1992). Toward a brain map of auditory hallucinations. *American Journal of Psychiatry, 149,* 1062–1069.

CNN. (2005, April 14). *Study seeks standard for sexual disorder. Retrieved 2/24/2004 from http://www.cnn.com.*

Compas, B. E., Haaga, D. A., Keefe, F. J., Leitenberg, H., & Williams, D. A. (1998). Sampling of empirically supported psychological treatments from health psychology: Smoking, chronic pain, cancer, and bulimia nervosa. *Journal of Consulting and Clinical Psychology, 66,* 89–112.

Conte, H. R., Plutchik, R., Wild, K. V., & Karasu, T. B. (1986). Combined psychotherapy and pharmacotherapy for depression: A systematic analysis of the evidence. *Archives of General Psychiatry, 43,* 471–479.

Cooper, W. O., Arbogast, P. G., Ding, H., Hickson, G. B., Fuchs, C., & Ray, W. A. (2006). Trends in prescribing of antipsychotic medications for US children. *Ambulatory Pediatrics, 6,* 79–83.

Corrigan, P. W. (1997). Behavior therapy empowers persons with severe mental illness. *Behavior Modification, 21,* 45–61.

Corrigan, P. W., & Holms, E. P. (1994). Patient identification of "street skills" for a psychosocial training module. *Hospital and Community Psychiatry, 45,* 273–276.

Coyne, J. C., Kessler, R. C., Tal, M., Trunbull, J., Wortman, C. B., & Greden, J. F. (1987). Living with a depressed person. *Journal of Consulting and Clinical Psychology, 55,* 347–352.

Creed, F., Fernandes, L., Guthrie, E., Palmer, S., Ratcliffe, J., Read, N., Rigby, C., Thompson, D., & Tomenson, B. (2003). The cost-effectiveness of psychotherapy and paroxetine for severe irritable bowel syndrome. *Gastroenterology, 124,* 303–317.

Dalton, K. (1987). What is PMS? In M. R. Walsh (Ed.), *The psychology of women: Ongoing debates.* (pp. 131–136). New Haven, CT: Yale University Press.

Davidson, J. R. T., et al. (2002). Effect of *hypericum perforatum* (Saint-John's wort) in major depressive disorder: A randomized controlled trial. *Journal of the American Medical Association, 287,* 1807–1814.

DeNoon, D. (2004, May 10). Paxil may help irritable bowel syndrome. Retrieved 11/18/2006 from *www.webmd.com/content/article/86/992242.htm.*

DeNoon, D. (2006, March 22). New hope for depression patients: Half of people with major depression get well after 1st of 2nd treatment. Retrieved 3/23/2006 from *http://www.webmd.com/content/article/120/113702.htm.*

Diamant, A. (1997). *The red tent.* New York: Picador.

Dickerson, F., Ringel, N., Parente, F., & Boronow, J. (1994). Seclusion and restraint, assaultiveness, and patient performance in a token economy. *Hospital and Community Psychiatry, 45,* 168–170.

Diller, L. H. (1998). *Running on Ritalin.* New York: Bantam Books.

Dingfelder, S. (2004, April). CBT may stabilize over-activity in higher-order brain areas. *Monitor on Psychology,* 11.

Dobson, D. J., McDougall, G., Busheikin, J., & Aldous, J. (1995). Effects of social skills training and social milieu treatment on symptoms of schizophrenia. *Psychiatric Services, 46,* 376–380.

Dobson, K. S. (1989). A meta-analysis of the efficacy of cognitive therapy for depression. *Journal of Consulting and Clinical Psychology, 57,* 414–419.

Drake, R. E., & Sederer, L. I. (1986). The adverse effects of intensive treatment of chronic schizophrenia. *Comprehensive Psychiatry, 27,* 313–326.

Dugas, M. J., Ladouceur, R., Leger, E., Freeston, M. H., Langolis, F., Provencher, M. D., & Boisvert, J. (2003). Group cognitive-behavioral therapy for generalized anxiety disorder: Treatment outcome and long-term follow-up. *Journal of Consulting and Clinical Psychology, 71,* 821–825.

Eisenberger, R. (1989). *Blue Monday: The loss of the work ethic in America.* New York: Paragon.

Eisenberger, R. (1992). Learned Industriousness. *Psychological Review, 99,* 248–267.

Elias, M. (2005, September 9). Number of adults on ADHD drugs doubles. Retrieved from *www.usatoday.com/news/health/2005–09–14– adhd-drugs-usage_x.htm.*

Elliott, C. (2006). The drug pushers. *Atlantic Monthly,* 82–93.

Ellis, A. (1993). Changing rational-emotive therapy (RET) to rational-emotive behavior therapy (REBT). *The Behavior Therapist, 16,* 257–258.

Esposito, K., Giugliano, F., Di Palo, C., Giugliano, G., Marfella, R., D'Andrea, F., D'Armiento, M., & Giugliano, D. (2004). Effect of lifestyle changes on erectile dysfunction in obese men. *Journal of the American Medical Association, 291,* 2978–2984.

Ezquiaga, E., Garcia, A., Pallares, T., & Bravo, M. F. (1999). Psychosocial predictors of outcome in major depression: A prospective 12-month study. *Journal of Affective Disorders, 52,* 209–216.

Fallon, A. E., & Rozin, P. (1985). Sex differences in perceptions of desirable body shape. *Journal of Abnormal Psychology, 94,* 102–105.

Falloon, I. R. H., Brooker, C., & Graham-Hole, V. (1992). Psychosocial interventions for schizophrenia. *Archives of General Psychology, 42,* 887–896.

Faraone, S. V. (2003, August). *ADHD: Facts and fiction.* Toronto, Canada: American Psychological Association Annual Convention.

Farrell, J. (2003, January 3). "Go pills" routine for U.S. pilots. *The Edmonton Journal,* p. 1.

Ferguson, C. P., La Via, M. C., Crossan, P. J., & Kaye, W. H. (1999). Are serotonin selective reuptake inhibitors effective in underweight anorexia nervosa? *International Journal of Eating Disorders, XX,* 11–17.

Flora, S. R. (2004). *The power of reinforcement..* Albany: State University of New York Press.

Flora, S. R., & Flora, D. B. (1999). Effects of extrinsic reinforcement for reading during childhood on reported reading habits of college students. *Psychological Record, 49,* 3–14.

Flora, S. R., & Popanak, S. S. (2004). Childhood pay for grades is related to college grade point averages. *Psychological Reports, 94,* 66.

Flora, S. R., & Sellers, M. (2003). "Premenstrual dysphoric disorder" and "premenstrual syndrome" myths. *Skeptical Inquirer, 27,* 37–42.

Foa, E. B., Kizak, M. J., & Liebowitz, M, et al. (1993). *Treatment of obsessive compulsive disorder by behavior therapy, clomipramine, and their combination: Preliminary results of a multi-center double-blind controlled trial.* Paper presented at the annual meeting of the Association for Advancement of Behavior Therapy, Atlanta, GA.

Franklin, M. E., Abramowitz, J. S., Bux, D. A., Zoellner, L. A., & Feeny, N. C. (2002). Cognitive-behavioral therapy with and without medication in the treatment of obsessive-compulsive disorder. *Professional Psychology: Research and Practice, 33,* 162–168.

Franklin, M. E., & Foa, E. B. (2002). Cognitive behavioral treatments for obsessive-compulsive disorder. In P. E. Nathan & J. M. Gorman (Eds.), *A guide to treatments that work* (pp. 367–410). New York: Oxford University Press.

Freeman, C. (1998). Drug treatment for bulimia nervosa. *Neuropsychobiology, 37,* 72–79.

Gadow, K. D. (1985). Relative efficacy of pharmacological behavioral and combination treatments for enhancing academic performance. *Clinical Psychology Review, 5,* 513–533.

Garcia, C., Micallef, J., Dubeuil, D., Philippot, P., Jouve, E., & Blin, O. (2000). Effects of lorazepam on emotional reactivity, performance, and vigilance in subjects with high or low anxiety. *Journal of Clinical Psychopharmacology, 20,* 226–233.

Gaudiano, B. A., & Herbert, J. D. (2006). Acute treatment of inpatients with psychotic symptoms using acceptance and commitment therapy: Pilot results. *Behavior Research and Therapy, 44,* 415–437.

Gelman, S. (1999). *Medicating schizophrenia: A history.* New Brunswick, NJ: Rutgers University Press.

GlaxoSmithKline. (2001). *Generalized anxiety disorder: When you can't stop the worry.* Company informational pamphlet.

Goodale, L., Domar, A., & Benson, H. (1990). Alleviation of premenstrual syndrome symptoms with the relaxation response. *Obstetrics and Gynecology, 74,* 649–655.

Gould, R. A., Otto, M. W., & Pollack, M. H. (1995). A meta-analysis of treatment outcome for panic disorder. *Clinical Psychology Review, 15,* 819–844.

Graedon, J., & Graedon, T. (2000a, January 6). Drug complications often go unreported. *Vindicator,* p. A4.

Graedon, J., & Graedon, T. (2000b, August 13). Try therapy for girl's shyness before resorting to medication. *Vindicator,* p. A12.

Greenberg, R. P., Bornstein, R. F., Greenberg, M. D., & Fisher, S. (1992). A meta-analysis of antidepressant outcome under "blinder" conditions. *Journal of Consulting and Clinical Psychology, 60,* 664–669.

Greenwald, D. P., Kornblith, S. J., Hersen, M., Bellack, A. S., & Himmelhoch, J. M. (1981). Differences between social skills, therapists, and psychotherapists in treating depression. *Journal of Consulting and Clinical Psychology, 49,* 757–759.

Grilo, C. M. (2001). Pharmacological and psychological treatments of obesity and binge eating disorder. In M. T. Sammons & N. B. Schmidt (Eds.), *Combined treatments for mental disorders* (pp.239–270). Washington, DC: American Psychological Association.

Grob, G. N. (1991). *From asylum to community: Mental health policy in modern America.* Princeton, NJ: Princeton University Press.

Guterman, L., & Van Der Werf, M. (2001 October 5). 12 journals adopt joint policy on research supported by business. *The Chronicle of Higher Education,* p. A29.

Harris, T., Brown, G. W., & Robinson, R. (1999). Befriending as an intervention for chronic depression among women in an inner city: 1: Randomized controlled trial. *British Journal of Psychiatry, 174,* 219–224.

Haug, T. T., Blomhoff, S., Hellstrom, K., Holme, I., Humble, M., Madsbu, H. P., & Wold, J. E. (2003). Exposure therapy and sertraline in social phobia: 1-year follow-up of a randomized controlled trial. *British Journal of Psychiatry, 182,* 312–318.

Hayes, S. C., Strosahl, K. D., & Wilson, K. G. (1999). *Acceptance and commitment therapy: An experiential approach to behavior change.* New York: Guilford Press.

Herzog, D. B., Keller, M. B., Strober, M., Yeh, C., & Pai, S. (1992). The current status of treatment for anorexia nervosa and bulimia nervosa. *International Journal of Eating Disorders, 12,* 215–220.

Hogarty, G. E., Anderson, C. M., Reiss, D. J., Kornblith, S. J., Greenwald, D. P., Ulrich, R. F., & Carter, M. (1991). Family psychoeducation, social skills training, and maintenance chemotherapy in the aftercare treatment of schizophrenia. *Archives of General Psychiatry, 48,* 340–347.

Hollon, S. D., Shelton, R. C., & Loosen, P. T. (1991). Cognitive therapy and pharmacotherapy for depression. *Journal of Consulting and Clinical Psychology, 59,* 88–99.

Hopko, D. R., Armento, M. E. A., Cantu, M. S., Chambers, L L., & Lejuez, C. W. (2003). The use of daily diaries to assess the relations amoung mood state, overt behavior, and reward value of activities. *Behavior Research and Therapy, 41,* 1137–1148.

Hopko, D. R., Lejuez, W. C., LePage, J. P., Hopko, S. D., & McNeil, D. W. (2003). A brief behavioral activation treatment for depression. *Behavior Modification, 27,* 458–469.

Horwitz, A. V. (2002). *Creating mental illness.* Chicago: University of Chicago Press.

Hupp, S. D. A., Reitman, D., Northup, J., O'Callaghan, & LeBlanc, M. (2002). The effects of delayed rewards, tokens, and stimulant medication on sportsmanlike behavior with ADHD-diagnosed children. *Behavior Modification, 26,* 148–162.

Jackson, H. J., Smith, N., & McCorry, P. (1990). Relationship between expressed emotion and family burden in psychotic disorders: An exploratory study. *Acta Psychiatrica Scandinavica, 82,* 243–249.

Jacobs, G. D., Pace-Schott, E. F., Stickgold, R., & Otto, M. W. (2004). Cognitive behavior therapy and pharmacotherapy for insomnia. *Archives of Internal Medicine, 164,* 1888–1896.

Jacobs, H. E., Collier, R., & Wissusik, D. (1992). The job-finding module: Training skills for seeking competitive community employment. *New Directions for Mental Health Services, 53,* 105–115.

Jacobson, N. S., & Gortner, E. T. (2000). Can depression be de-medicalized in the 21st century: Scientific revolutions, counter-revolutions, and the magnetic field of normal science. *Behavior Research and Therapy, 38,* 103–117.

Jacobson, N. S., Martell, C. R., & Dimidjian, S. (2001). Behavioral activation treatment for depression: Returning to contextual roots. *Clinical Psychology: Science and Practice, 8,* 255–270.

Jansen, A. (2001). Towards effective treatment of eating disorders: Nothing is as practical as a good theory. *Behavior Research and Therapy, 39,* 1007–1022.

Johnson, W. G., Tosh, J. Y., & Varnado, P. J. (1996). Eating disorders: Efficacy of pharmacological and psychological interventions. *Clinical Psychology Review, 16,* 457–478.

Kampman, M. Keijsers, G. P. J., Hoogduin, C. A. L., & Verbraak, M. J. P. M. (2002). Addition of cognitive behavior therapy for obsessive-compulsive disorder patients non-responding to fluoxetine. *Acta Psychiatrica Scandinavica, 106,* 314–319.

Keefer, L., & Blanchard, E. B. (2001). The effects of relaxation response meditation on the symptoms of irritable bowel syndrome: Results of a controlled treatment study. *Behavior Research and Therapy, 39,* 801–811.

Kelley, H. H., & Thibaut, J. W. (1978). *Interpersonal relations.* New York: Wiley.

Kelly, J. B. (1998). Marital conflict, divorce, and children's adjustment. *Child and Adolescent Psychiatric Clinics of North America, 7,* 259–271.

Kessler, R. C. (1997). The effect of stressful life events on depression. *Annual Review of Psychology, 48,* 191–214.

Khan, A., Khan, S., & Brown, W. A. (2002). Are placebo controls necessary to test new antidepressants and anxiolytics? *International Journal of Neuropsychopharmacology, 5,* 193–197.

Kingdon, D. G., & Turkington, D. (1991). The use of cognitive behavior therapy with a normalizing rationale in schizophrenia. *Journal of Nervous and Mental Disease, 179,* 207–211.

Kirby, R. (1994). Changes in premenstrual symptoms and irrational thinking following cognitive-behavioral coping skills training. *Journal of Consulting and Clinical Psychology, 62,* 1026–1032.

Kirsch, I., Moore, T. J., Scoboria, A., & Nicholls, S. S. (2002). The emperor's new drugs: An analysis of antidepressant medication data submitted to the U.S. Food and Drug Administration. *Prevention and Treatment, 5,* 40–50.

Klein, K. B. (1988). Controlled treatment trials on the irritable bowel syndrome: A critique. *Gastroenterology, 95,* 232–241.

Koerner, B. I. (2002, July–August). Disorders made to order. *Mother Jones,* 58–81.

Kollins, S. H., MacDonald, E. K., & Rush, C. R. (2001). Assessing the abuse potential of methylphenidate in nonhuman and human subjects. *Pharmacology, Biochemistry, and Behavior, 68,* 611–627.

Kravitz, R. L., Epstein, R. M., Feldman, M.D., et al. (2005). Influence of patients' requests for direct-to-consumer advertised antidepressants. *Journal of the American Medical Association, 293,* 1949.

Lam, J. N., & Steketee, G. S. (2001). Reducing obsessions and compulsions through behavior therapy. *Psychoanalytic Inquiry, 21,* 157–182.

Laties, V. G., & Weiss, B. (1981). The amphetamine margin in sports. *Federation Proceedings, 40,* 2689–2692.

Laumann, E. O., Paik, A., & Rosen, C. (1999). Sexual dysfunction in the United States: Prevalence and predictors. *Journal of the American Medical Association, 281,* 537–544.

LaValle, D. (1994). Social exchange and social system: A Parsonian approach. *Sociological Perspectives, 37,* 585–610.

Lewinsohn, P. M. (1974). A behavioral approach to depression. In R. J. Friedman & M. M. Katz (Eds.), *The psychology of depression: Contemporary theory and research* (pp. 157-185). Washington, DC: Winston-Wiley.

Lewinsohn, P. M., Gotlib, I. H., & Seeley, J. R. (1997). Depression-related psychosocial variables: Are they specific to depression in adolescents? *Journal of Abnormal Psychology, 106*, 365–376.

Liberman, R. P., & Corrigan, P. W. (1993). Designing new psychosocial treatments for schizophrenia. *Psychiatry, 56*, 238–249.

Liberman, R. P., Teigen, J., Patterson, R., & Baker, V. (1973). Reducing delusional speech in chronic, paranoid schizophrenics. *Journal of Applied Behavior Analysis, 6*, 57–64.

Linn, M. W., Klett, C. J., & Caffey, E. M. (1980). Foster home characteristics and psychiatric patient outcome. *Archives of General Psychiatry, 37*, 129–132.

Marvan, M. L., & Cortes-Iniestra, S. (2001). Women's beliefs about the prevalence of premenstrual syndrome and biases in recall of premenstrual changes. *Health Psychology, 20*, 276–280.

Marvan, M. L., & Escobedo, C. (1999). Premenstrual symptomatology: Role of prior knowledge about premenstrual syndrome. *Psychosomatic Medicine, 61*, 163–167.

Masters, W. H., & Johnson, V. E. (1966). *Human sexual inadequacy.* Boston: Little, Brown.

McDowell, J. J. (1982). The importance of Hernstein's mathematical statement of the law of effect for behavior therapy. *American Psychology, 37*, 771–779.

McGuire, P. K., Shah, G. M. S., & Murray, R. M. (1993). Increased blood flow in Broca's area during auditory hallucinations in schizophrenia. *Lancet, 342*, 703–706.

McNally, S. E., & Goldberg, J. O. (1997). Natural cognitive coping strategies in schizophrenia. *British Journal of Medical Psychology, 70* (Pt. 2), 159–167.

Mello, M. M., Clarridge, B. R., & Studdert, D. M. (2005). Academic medical centers' standards for clinical-trial agreements with industry. *The New England Journal of Medicine, 352*, 2202–2210.

Meyer, M. (2000, December 17). There's help for social phobia. *Parade*, 10–11.

Miller, G. (2003, January 4). "Go" pills for F-16 pilots get close look: Amphetamines prescribed in mission that killed Canadians. *San Francisco Chronicle*, p. 1.

Mitchell, J. E., Pyle, E. L., Eckert, E. D., Hatsukami, D., Pomeroy, C., & Zimmerman, R. (1990). A comparison study of antidepressants and structured intensive group psychotherapy in the treatment of bulimia nervosa. *Archives of General Psychiatry, 47*, 149–157.

Molm, L. D. (1994). Dependence and risk: Transforming the structure of social exchange. *Social Psychology Quarterly, 57,* 163–176.

Moos, R. H. (1974). *Evaluating treatment environments: A social-ecological approach.* New York: Wiley.

Morgenstern, H., & Glazer, W. M. (1993). Identifying risk factors for tardive dyskinesia among long-term outpatients maintained with neuroleptic medications: Results of the Yale tardive dyskinesia study. *Archives of General Psychiatry, 50,* 723–733.

Moss, H. B., Panzak, G. L., & Tarter, R. E. (1993). Sexual functioning of male anabolic steroid abusers. *Archives of Sexual Behavior, 22,* 1–12.

MTA Cooperative Group. (1999). Fourteen-month randomized clinical trial of treatment stategies for attention-deficit hyperactivity disorder. *Archives of General Psychiatry, 56,* 1073–1086.

Nangle, D. W., Erdley, C. A., Newman, J. E., Mason, C. A., & Carpenter, E. M. (2003). Popularity, friendship quantity, and friendship quality: Interactive influences on children's loneliness and depression. *Journal of Clinical Child and Adolescent Psychology, 32,* 546–555.

Nichols, K. (2004, December 17). The other performance-enhancing drugs. *The Chronicle of Higher Education,* pp. A16–A17.

Nicholson, S. (2004, March 13). Drug counselor: Prevention is key. *Charlotte Observer,* p. 5b.

Nolan, E. D., Gadow, K. D., & Sprafkin J. (2001). Teacher reports of DSM-IV ADHD, ODD, and CD symptoms in schoolchildren. *Journal of American Academy of Child & Adolescent Psychiatry, 40,* 241–249.

O'Sullivan, G., Noshirvani, H., Marks, I., Monteiro, W., & Lelliott, P. (1991). Six-year follow-up after exposure and clomipramine therapy for obsessive-compulsive disorder. *Journal of Clinical Psychiatry, 52,* 150–155.

Otho-McNeil (2004, May 10). *Who wants to talk about premature ejaculation?* San Francisco: Otho-McNeil.

Palmstierna, T., Huifeldt, B., & Wistedt B., (1991). The relationship of crowding and aggressive behavior on a psychiatric intensive care unit. *Hospital and Community Psychiatry, 42,* 1237–1240.

Patrick, D. L., Althof, S. E., Pryor, J. I., Rosen, R., Rowland, D. L., Ho, K. F., et al. (2005). Premature ejaculation: An observational study of men and their partners. *Journal of Sexual Medicine, 2,* 358.

Paul, G. L., & Lentz, R. J. (1977). *Psychosocial treatment of chronic mental patients: Milieu versus social learning programs.* Cambridge, MA: Harvard University Press.

Pearlstein, T., & Steiner, M. (2000). Non-antidepressant treatment of premenstrual syndrome. *Journal of Clinical Psychiatry, 61,* 22–27.

Pelham, W. E. (1999). The NIMH multimodal treatment study for attention-deficit hyperactivity disorder: Just say yes to drugs alone? *Canadian Journal of Psychiatry, 44,* 981–990.

Pelham, W. E., Gangy, E. M., Greiner, A. R., Hoza, B., Hinshaw, S. P., Swanson, J. M., Simpson, S., Shapiro, C., Bukstein, O., Baron-Myak, C., & McBurnett, K. (2000). Behavioral versus behavioral and pharmacological treatment in ADHD children attending a summer treatment program. *Journal of Abnormal Child Psychology, 28,* 507–525.

Phillips, E. L., Phillips, E. A., Fixsen, D. L., & Wolf, M. M. (1971). Achievement place: Modification of the behaviors of pre-delinquent boys within a token economy. *Journal of Applied Behavior Analysis, 4,* 45–59.

Pierce, W. D., & Epling, W. F. (1994). Activity anorexia: An interplay between basic and applied behavior analysis. *Behavior Analyst, 17,* 7–23.

Pike, K., M., Walsh, B. T., Vitousek, K., Wilson, G., T., & Bauer, J. (2003). Cognitive behavior therapy in the posthospitalization treatment of anorexia nervosa. *American Journal of Psychiatry, 160,* 2046–2049.

Rachlin, H. (1991). *Introduction to modern behaviorism* (3rd ed.). New York: Freeman.

Ray, W. A., Gurwitz, J., Decker, M., & Kennedy, D. L. (1992). Medications and the safety of the older driver: Is there a basis for concern? *Human Factors, 34,* 33–47.

Readers Digest (2001, June). *Prescription Drug Use Rises.* 38.

Red Herring. (2005, May 24). *Premature ejaculation drug: Johnson & Johnson announces successful pivotal trial results for a drug to treat premature ejaculation.* Retrieved 3/27/2006 from http://www.redherring.com

Reisinger, J. J. (1972). The treatment of "anxiety-depression" via positive reinforcement and response cost. *Journal of Applied Behavior Analysis, 5,* 125–130.

Reitman, D., Hupp, S. D. A., O'Callaghan, P. M., Gulley, V., & Northup, J. (2001). The influence of a token economy and methylphenidate on attentive and disruptive behavior during sports with children ADHD-diagnosed children. *Behavior Modification, 25,* 305–323.

Ricca, V., Mannucci, E., Mezzani, B., Moretti, S., Di Bernardo, M., Bertelli, M., Rotella, C. M., & Faravelli, C. (2001). Fluoxetine and fluvoxamine combined with individual cognitive-behavior therapy in binge eating disorder: A one-year follow-up study. *Psychotherapy and Psychosomatics, 70,* 298–306.

Rickels, K., Zaninelli, R., McCafferty, J., Bellew, K., Lyengar, M., & Sheehan, D. (2003). Paroxetine treatment of generalized anxiety disorder: A double-blind, placebo-controlled study. *American Journal of Psychiatry, 160,* 749–756.

Robin, A. L., Gilroy, M., & Dennis, A. B. (1998). Treatment of eating disorders in children and adolescents. *Clinical Psychology Review, 18,* 421–446.

Rosack, J. (2004, December 3). Sleep experts wake up to value of CBT for insomnia. *Psychiatric News, 39,* 32.

Rosenthal, M. B., Berndt, E. R., Donohue, J. M., Frank, R. G., & Epstein, A. M. (2002). Promotion of prescription drugs to consumers. *The New England Journal of Medicine, 346,* 498–505.

Roy-Byrne, P. P., & Cowley, D. S. (2002). Pharmacological treatments for panic disorder, generalized anxiety disorder, specific phobia, and social anxiety disorder. In P. E. Nathan & J. M. Gorman (Eds.), *A guide to treatments that work* (pp. 337–366).New York: Oxford University Press.

Rubin, R. (2006, March 22). Panel: ADHD drugs for kids need hallucination warning. *Retrieved 3/27/2005 from http://www.*usatoday.com 1–2.

Rush, A. J., Trivedi, M. H., Wisniewski, S. R., et al. (2006). Bupropion-SR, Sertraline, or Venlafaxine-XR after failure of SSRIs for depression. *The New England Journal of Medicine, 354,* 1231–1242.

Salkovskis, P. M., & Campbell, P. (1994). Thought suppression induces intrusion in naturally occurring negative intrusive thoughts. *Behavior Research and Therapy, 32,* 1–8.

Sammons, M. T., & Schmidt, N. B. (2001). *Combined treatments for mental disorders: A guide to psychological and pharmacological intervention.* Washington, DC: American Psychological Association.

Satterfield, J. H., Hoppe, C., & Schell, A. (1982). A prospective study of delinquency in 110 adolescent boys with attention-deficit disorder and 88 normal adolescent boys. *American Journal of Psychiatry, 139,* 795–798.

Satterfield, J. H., Satterfield, B. T., & Schell, A. M. (1987). Therapeutic interventions to prevent delinquency in hyperactive boys. *Journal of the American Academy of Child and Adolescent Psychiatry, 26,* 56–64.

Satterfield, J. H., & Schell, A. (1997). A prospective study of hyperactive boys with conduct problems and normal boys: Adolescent and adult criminality. *Journal of the American Academy of Child and Adolescent Psychiatry, 36,* 1726–1735.

Sax, L., & Kautz, K. J. (2003). Who suggests the diagnosis of attention-deficit/hyperactivity disorder? *Annals of Family Medicine, 1,* 171–174.

Schmidt, N. B., Koselka, M., & Woolaway-Bickel, K. (2001). Combined treatments for phobic anxiety disorders. In M. T. Sammons & N. B. Schmidt (Eds.), *Combined treatments for mental disorders (pp. 81–110)*. Washington, DC: American Psychological Association.

Schmidt, O. (2005). Talk it up. *Scientific American Mind, 16*, 90–91.

Schwartz, J. M., Stossel, P. W., Baxter, L. R., Martin, K. M., & Phelps, M. E. (1996). Systematic changes in cerebral glucose metabolic rate after successful behavior modification treatment of obsessive-compulsive disorder. *Archives of General Psychiatry, 53*, 109–113.

Schwartz, S. (2000). *Abnormal psychology*. Mountain View, CA: Mayfield.

Seligman, M. E. P. (1975). *Helplessness: On depression, development, and death*. San Francisco: Freeman.

Shea, S. E., Gordon, K., Hawkins, A., Kawchuk, J., & Smith, D. (2000, December 12). Pathology in the Hundred Acre Wood: A neurodevelopmental perspective on A. A. Milne. *CMAJ: Canadian Medical Association Journal, 163*, 1557–1560.

Sheeber, L., Hops, H., Andrews, J., Alpert, T., & Davis, B. (1998). Interactional processes in families with depressed and non-depressed adolescents: Reinforcement of depressive behavior. *Behavior Research and Therapy, 36*, 417–427.

Shute, N., Locy, T., & Pasternak, D. (2000, March 6). The perils of pills. *U.S. News & World Report*, 44–50.

Skinner, B. F. (1953). *Science and human behavior*. New York: Macmillan.

Skinner, B. F., & Vaughan, M. E. (1987). *Enjoy old age*. New York: Norton.

Sloan, R. B., Staples, F. R., Cristol, A. H., Yorkston, N. J., & Whipple, K. (1975). *Psychotherapy versus behavior therapy*. Cambridge, MA: Harvard University Press.

Smith, D. (2002, March). Placebo alters brain function of people with depression. *Monitor on Psychology*, 16.

Smith, M. (2005, July 1). FDA reviews adult antidepressant-suicide link. Retrieved 11/18/2006 from *http://www.webmd.com/content/article/108/108778.htm*

Sommers, C. H. (2000). *The war against boys*. New York: Simon & Schuster.

Soukhanov, A. H. (Ed.) (1992). *American Heritage Dictionary of the English Language*. (3rd. ed.). Boston, MA: Houghton Mifflin.

Stanley, M. A., Beck, J. G., Novy, D. M., Averill, P. M., Swann, A. C., Diefenbach, G. J., & Hopko, D. R. (2003). Cognitive-behavioral treatment of late-life generalized anxiety disorder. *Journal of Consulting and Clinical Psychology, 71,* 309–319.

Stein, D. B. (1999). *Ritalin is not the answer.* San Francisco: Jossey-Bass.

Steiner, M. S., Steinberg, D., Stewart, D., Carter, C., Berger, & R. Reid, et al. (1995). Flouxetine in the treatment of premenstrual dysphoria. *The New England Journal of Medicine, 332.* 1529–1534.

Steinbrueck, S. M., Maxwell, S. E., & Howard, G. S. (1983). A meta-analysis of psychotherapy and drug therapy in the treatment of unipolar depression with adults. *Journal of Consulting and Clinical Psychology, 51,* 856–863.

Stoddard, J. L. (1999). The effect of moderate aerobic exercise on premenstrual distress and ovarian steroid hormones. *Dissertation Abstracts International: Section B: The Sciences and Engineering, 60,* 2641.

Sykes, M. A., Blanchard, E. B., Lackner, J., Keefer, L., & Krasner, S. (2003). Psychopathology in irritable bowel syndrome: Support for a psychophysiological model. *Journal of Behavioral Medicine, 26,* 361–372.

Task Force on Promotion and Dissemination of Psychological Procedures (1995). Training in and dissemination of empirically-validated psychological treatments: report and recommendationa. *The Clinical Psychologist, 48,* 3–23.

Tavris, C. (1992). *The mismeasure of woman.* New York: Simon & Schuster.

Tavris, C. (2001). *Psychobabble and biobunk.* Upper Saddle River, NJ: Prentice Hall.

Taylor, D. (1999). Effectiveness of professional-peer group treatment: Symptom management for women with PMS. *Research in Nursing and Health, 22,* 496–511.

Thase, M. E. (1990). Relapse and recurrence in unipolar major depression: Short-term and long-term approaches. *Journal of Clinical Psychiatry, 51* (6, Suppl.), 51–57.

Thompson, M. L., & Gick, M. L. (2000). Medical care-seeking for menstrual symptoms. *Journal of Psychosomatic Research, 49,* 137–140.

Thom, A., Sartory, G., & Johren, P. (2000). Comparison between one-session psychological treatment and benzodiazepine in dental phobia. *Journal of Consulting and Clinical Psychology, 68,* 378–387.

Tirch, D., & Radnitz, C. L. (1997). Cognitive behavioral treatment of irritable bowel syndrome. *The Clinical Psychologist, 50,* 18–20.

Tkachuk, G. A. (1999, December). Health: Jog your mood. *Psychology Today,* 24.

Tkachuk, G. A., Graff, L. A., Martin, G. L., & Bernstein, C. N. (2003). Randomized controlled trial of cognitive-behavioral group therapy for irritable bowel syndrome in a medical setting. *Journal of Clinical Psychology in Medical Settings, 10,* 57–69.

Tkachuk, G. A., & Martin, G. L. (1999). Exercise therapy for patients with psychiatric disorders: Research and clinical implication. *Professional Psychology: Research & Practive, 30,* 275–282.

Trower, P. (1982). Toward a generative model of social skills: A critique and synthesis. In J. P. Curran & P. M. Monti (Eds.), *Social skills training: A practical handbook for assessment and treatment* (pp. 399–428). New York: Guilford.

Umbricht, D., & Kane, J. M. (1996). Medical complications of new antipsychotic drugs. *Schizophrenia Bulletin, 22,* 475–483.

van Balkon, A. J. L. M., de Haan, E., van Oppen, P., Spinhoven, P., Hoogduin, K. A. L., & van Dyck, R. (1997, May). *Cognitive behavioral therapy versus the combination with fluvoxamine in the treatment of obsessive compulsive disorder.* Paper presented at the meeting of the American Psychiatric Association, San Diego, CA.

Vonk, M. E., & Thyer, B. A. (1995). Exposure therapy in the treatment of vaginal penetration phobia: A single-case evaluation. *Journal of Behavioral Therapy and Experimental Psychiatry, 26,* 359–363.

Wallace, C. , Liberman, R. P., MacKain, S. J., Blackwell, G., & Eckman, T. A. (1992). Effectiveness and replicability of modules for teaching social and instrumental skills to the severely mentally ill. *American Journal of Psychiatry, 149,* 654–658.

Wallis, C. (1994, July 18). Life in overdrive. *Time,* 42–48.

Warren, R., & Thomas, J. C. (2001). Cognitive-behavior therapy of obsessive-complusive disorder in private practice: An effectiveness study. *Anxiety Disorders, 15,* 277–285.

Weber, R. L. (2004, November 30). A drug kids take in search of better grades. *The Christian Science Monitor,* pp. 1–3.

Weiden, P. J., Dixion, L., Frances, A., Appelbaum, P., Haas, G., & Rapkin, B. (1991). In C. A. Tamminga & S. C. Schulz (Eds.), *Advances in neuropsychiatry and psychopharmacology. 1: Schizophrenia research* (pp. 285–296). New York: Raven Press.

Weisz, J. R., & Hawley, K. M. (1998). Finding, evaluating, refining, and applying empirically supported treatments for children and adolescents. *Journal of Clinical Child Psychology, 27,* 206–216.

Wexler, B. E., & Cicchetti, D. V. (1992). The outpatient treatment of depression: Implications of outcome research for clinical practice. *The Journal of Nervous and Mental Disease, 180*(5), 277–286.

Whitehead, W. E., Crowell, M. D., Heller, B. R., Robinson, J. C., Schuster, M. M., & Horn, S. (1994). Modeling and reinforcement of the sick role during childhood predicts adult illness behavior. *Psychosomatic Medicine, 56,* 541–550.

Wilder, D. A., Masuda, A., O'Connor, C., & Baham, M. (2001). Brief functional analysis and treatment of bizarre vocalizations in an adult with schizophrenia. *Journal of Applied Behavior Analysis, 34,* 65–68.

Wilson, G. T. (1981). The effect of alcohol on human sexual behavior. In N. Mello (Ed.), *Advances on substance abuse: Behavioral and biological research* (pp.1–40). Greenwich, CT: JAI Press.

Wilson, G. T., & Fairburn, C. G. (2002). Treatments for eating disorders. In P. E. Nathan & J. M. Gorman (Eds.), *A guide to treatments that work* (pp.) New York: Oxford University Press.

Winett, R. A., & Winkler, R. C. (1972). Current behavior modification in the classroom: Be still, be quiet, be docile. *Journal of Applied Behavior Analysis, 5,* 499–504.

Wolpe, J. (1981). Behavior therapy versus psychoanalysis. *American Psychologist, 36,* 159–164.

Zito, J. M., Safer, D. J., dosReis, S., Gardner, J. F., Boles, M. L, & Lynch, (2000). Trends in the prescribing of psychotropic medications to preschoolers. *JAMA: Journal of the American Medical Association, 283,*1025–1030.

Zwillich, T. (2005a, March 29). U.S. sleep problems getting worse. Retrived 11/18/2006 from *http://www.webmd.com/content/article/102/106923.htm*

Zwillich, T. (2005b, June 30). FDA to go slow on ADHD drug warnings. Retrieved 11/18/2006 from *http://www.webmd.com/content/article/108/108767.htm.*

Name Index

Subject Index

Need a Little Help
LAUNCHING YOUR ENCORE?

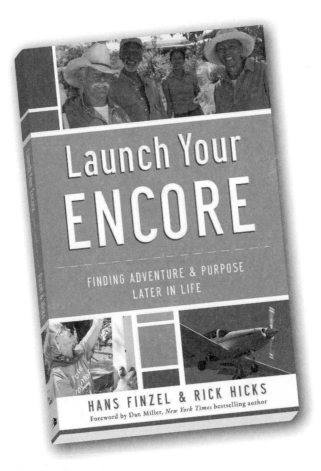

For additional resources and to learn about
Launch Your Encore seminars, please visit:

www.launchyourencore.com

a division of Baker Publishing Group
www.BakerBooks.com

Available wherever books are sold.